The Ginny Suite
Stacy Skolnik

Montez Press

Stacy Skolnik, The Ginny Suite
Second edition, 2024

© 2024 Stacy Skolnik & Montez Press
All rights reserved. No part of this publication
may be reproduced without permission in
writing by the author and the publisher.

Editors: Hasti, Emily Pope
Copy Editor: Rosanna McLaughlin
Graphic Design: JMMP – Julian Mader, Max Prediger
Print: DZA Druckerei zu Altenburg
Edition: 500

Montez Press Ltd.
Unit 29, Penarth Centre
Penarth Street
SE15 1TR, London
United Kingdom

ISBN: 978-3-945247-34-1

www.montezpress.com
@montezpress

The Ginny Suite

Stacy Skolnik

> Advertisement
>
> ## *So many clouds — one Memory FlashSystem*®

06:33AM EDT | 19,294 VIEWS

New Syndrome Remains Unexplained as First Known East Coast Cases Are Reported

JESSE L. SUTTON | CONTRIBUTOR

NEW YORK—First identified five months ago in California, cases of the new syndrome that continues to baffle doctors have since surfaced in Canada, Hawaii, Japan, Russia, France, Germany, the United Kingdom, and now New York. The constellation of inexplicable sensory experiences and physical symptoms known as Sunnyvale syndrome has sickened thousands of women across the globe.

American researchers say they have identified the first known East Coast cases of the syndrome, inspiring fears that the illness is readily spread by humans, despite no evidence of contagion. While the condition has not been tied to any deaths, health officials in America and elsewhere are watching it carefully, and alerting the public, in an effort to help identify additional cases and ensure it does not develop into something more severe.

The incidents, the first of which was reported in Sunnyvale, California last October, have been controversial from the start. The onset of the syndrome typically presents with victims, either suddenly or over the course of weeks, experiencing difficulty with both speaking and understanding speech, as well as with reading or writing, before suffering other symptoms typically correlated to dissociative identity disorder. Some have dismissed the incidents as psychogenic illness, otherwise known as mass hysteria.

Doctors investigating the illness believe that many cases have gone undetected because of the lack of consensus regarding diagnostic criteria for identity disorders, and the difficulty even mental health professionals may have in diagnosing them.

Advertisement

Come along! Join us! Shop now!

Dr. Patricia Bevan of the New York University Medical Center said in an interview yesterday that she knew of 36 cases of dissociative identity disorder diagnosed in the last three weeks, but that it was unclear how many of these cases are connected to the new syndrome. In a letter informing other physicians of her findings, Dr. Bevan described the appearance of the outbreak as "rather confounding."

There is no national registry of dissociative identity disorder sufferers, but according to the National Alliance on Mental Illness, "up to 75% of people experience at least one depersonalization/derealization episode in their lives, with only 2% meeting the full criteria for chronic episodes." While women are more likely than men to be diagnosed with a dissociative disorder, in recent cases globally, doctors have been diagnosing Sunnyvale syndrome exclusively among women.

Advertisement

No more hiding. Feel free with luminous, wrinkle-free skin.

Although the ages of patients have ranged from 12 to 66 years, most have been under 40. In addition to typical indications of dissociative identity disorder such as amnesia and "out-of-body" experiences, many of the patients are also exhibiting symptoms such as narcolepsy and a condition known as illeism, in which speakers refer to themselves in the third person. What victims say begins as aphasia, nausea, and intense fatigue is often later accompanied by symptoms associated with catatonia, such as waxy flexibility and decreased sensitivity to pain.

According to Bevan, the reporting doctors said that most cases have involved heterosexual women who have undergone surgery for other medical conditions within the past year and a half.

Dr. Bevan said she had tested three of the victims and found severe mutations in positional candidate genes on chromosome channels expressed exclusively in the brain.

Analyses revealed that these structural mutations result in conformational changes of the mutant protein, which are suspected of leading to acute psychotic episodes of hallucination and derealization, while successive episodes may lead to increasingly severe catatonic residual states. Possible causes for this mutation have yet to be confirmed.

Dissociation is not believed to be contagious, but conditions that might precipitate it, such as environmental factors or certain viruses, could account for an outbreak among a single group.

Dr. Bevan, however, stated there was no apparent danger to women from contagion. "The best evidence against contagion," she said, "is that no cases have been reported to date among males."

Degenerate Matter

"I'll wait for you outside."

It's twenty degrees, smells like snow, and he's good on his dumb word. We hug awkwardly, and I get that familiar first date feeling like we're already mad at each other about something that hasn't happened yet. "You could have gone in...it's freezing."

"I know, but I said I'd wait outside."

"I know, but..."

He buys the first, second, and third rounds. I offer nothing, not because it's cash-only, but because I've learned my lesson. A few months ago, I became addicted to a scumbag who let me pay for every drink, sandwich, cigarette, and even a Chinatown bus from Atlanta where he said he'd been visiting a cousin, but I knew it was an ex. He never hit me up again after he got back. Money is just dirty paper, but it does set a precedent.

The stools we're sitting on are wobbly; my balance wanes with every sip. The wind threatens to knock me over whenever the door opens. Tells me to sit up straight, like a real doll.

He leans in close and whispers in my ear as if to say something sexy. "She's about to cry. The girl behind you." I don't look.

Forty minutes later. "Still might burst into tears."

As a child, like many children I hope to think, I went through a phase of morbid curiosity, spontaneous human combustion being one of my many subjects of interest, along with mutism and Tourette's syndrome, two sides of the same coin. I thought that if I could educate myself on the symptoms of a certain disorder thoroughly enough, I might be able to convince my family and friends and teachers of my suffering and relish their sympathies. I didn't want to experience any pain, though, which was one of the reasons I never resorted to cutting. It seemed too ubiquitous anyway, and I wanted whatever I didn't have to make me special. The rare, potentially pre-cancerous growth on my scalp that I was born with wouldn't do, as I wanted my self-selected condition to be something that would make me not grotesque and exposed, but beautiful and mysterious, fragile and feminine. I read that Victorian women aestheticized death as they paled their cheeks with powder and tightened their corsets to emulate the symptoms of tuberculosis, and I considered taking a similar approach. But at heart I knew I didn't have the self-control required to achieve a heroin-chic waifishness or anorexic pallor.

Of course, in retrospect, I'm haunted by this juvenile pursuit, karma eventually coming back around to kiss me on the forehead with a light case of hypochondria. But at the time, I wanted to be doted on, cared for more carefully because, I suppose, my loneliness made me desperate on those long evenings after school when I'd let myself in, pour myself some milk and sit down with a stack of three Oreos at the kitchen table to savor one half at a time, part of which I dropped to the bottom of my cup first, so it could bloat and disintegrate while I, plotting, enjoyed the rest.

It needed to be something I could fake, or something that would take me fast and easy, while simultaneously leaving behind an element of mystique, lore, to be cited in textbooks as a case story for years to come. At the library, I researched spontaneous human combustion, so unbelievable, almost mythological, but seemingly within the realm of plausibility. Something about it was comforting, a justification for the uneasy hum I felt brewing in my belly. It reminded me of what we'd read aloud in Sunday school. *Everything that can endure fire, you shall put through the fire, and it shall be clean.* Maybe one day my dad would walk into my room to find my body bursting into flames, disintegrating into ash, the seat of my desk chair charred, severed feet still smoking inside my beat-up All Stars, homework not yet finished.

While most of my research discredited it as pseudoscience, I sensed possibility, and sensing that, I figured it must be real. I never had a great vocabulary and I fared poorly in science but, like all women, I've always had my intuition. Inexpressible "gut feelings" swirling with fury in the chaotic intersection between my mouth and groin, my stomach a vat of irrational, suspicious, unspeakable things. That intuition would prove to be my ultimate affliction, the reason why I was so familiar with the recurring public embarrassment and slow drown of bursting, not into flames, but tears.

"I can relate," I tell him. "For as long as I can remember, almost every emotion for me has expressed itself through crying. Joy, frustration, guilt..."

I stop speaking as he looks at me with widened eyes and a frantic, kind of psychotic smile, nodding his head in a tic-like movement back towards her again.

Okay.

I swivel my seat around, pretending to look at the ceramic, or maybe plastic, Greek-style bust of a woman protruding from the wall like the head of a deer. Soft smile, wavy locks in a half pony, the lower strands falling over each shoulder. My eyes land on hers. I stay there for too long. They're filled to the brink and resentful of my stare.

Shame. That's one emotion that doesn't make me cry. I'm too busy pretending to be someone else.

I raise my drink, vodka celery something, and suck from my little red straw, cheeks puckering in at the sides like a fish.

He made me do it. Whatever you're crying about, blame him.

∽

Enough time has passed, and we want to make out but somehow I always end up on dates with guys that live outside the city, or with their parents, or have no home at all. This one lives two hours away on the Amtrak. So we book a car to a place where the lights don't turn on. It's nearly midnight and nothing is playing except for a horror with the word knives in the title.

His legs are in the shape of a V around mine, which are pressed together in the shape of an I. Or an H without the middle, collapsing.

I want to see the horror because I'm interested in understanding how to write one. But he describes the plot like a board game and I already know how it ends. I cancel the car.

Is that your dick on my leg? I don't ask. Instead, I say, "I'm hungry."

We walk a few blocks with his arm around my shoulder. The weight of his limb presses down on me oppressively, and I find myself struggling to stand up straight, like I struggled on the bar stool. Why is it so difficult to be a person with a body? The pain accumulating into a mass. Kind of ridiculous, the way we drag our sacks of flesh around from here to there, suspending our disbelief, larping inside our choices as if anything we do matters, as if we aren't all dirtying our shoes along the same forest's dark path. Like, what's even the point of this date I'm on? Best case scenario, it will reach a six-second pinnacle with a shudder of sensation. I guess the goal is to either become numb or to feel things so strongly you forget, for a few moments, you have a body. Or a mind.

The air is thin and cold, brittle; my breath appears before me and turns invisible again. A guy who talked too much told me recently, as I wavered in long, unsteady strides against the headlights of paused traffic on a night, for all intents and purposes, identical to this one, that the ancient Greeks used to think that breath was a mixture of air and fire, the essence of life, a bodily force that connected us with the cosmos. They thought our breath contained elements of our soul and the soul of Zeus too. The philosophers figured that if we need to breathe to live, then what we breathe must give us life, so the substance of our souls (whatever those are) must be air. He explained, as if he had developed the theory himself, that we "draw in Divine Reason through respiration, and therefore become thinking creatures."

"You've obviously never met the people I work with," I replied, even though it was too early in the night to sound so embittered.

Despite the fact that every icy inhalation tickles my throat and threatens a cough, seeing my soul naked before me in the form of condensation leaves me desperate for a cigarette. Maybe I'm an addict, or maybe it's a cosmic twinge, a longing for more of that age-old air and fire combo. But my hands are too cold. I'm all stiff and tangled up in his clutch. I'm not dressed warmly enough, and he teases me for it. I'm just a bitch in a leather skirt. The weather pinches through my tights.

"Oh, this place has food," I say, pointing across the street and looking up at him for permission.

"What's it called?"

I can't remember, which is ironic because it's Forgetmenot's and strange because it's directly underneath my office. I walk past it every day. Instead of answering, I cross the street with the awareness that he'll follow. The name doesn't matter and it's too cold to stand outside deliberating the way one does in an actual relationship when small choices become endurance exercises, heavy with the gravitas of unity. Or with prudence as a way to kill time.

Inside smells of mold and stale beer. A graveyard of bygone first dates. It's comforting.

"One martini and one Hoegaarden. Is that how you pronounce it? Hoe garden?"

"No. Who."

We eat wings and suck on our fingers until two a.m.

As I said, I work upstairs. It's the closest privacy I have keys to.

~

When we get to the office, I light a cigarette on the fire escape, and he joins me outside but doesn't smoke. We stare at each other over the course of a few drags. Every once in a while I look at my feet, glancing away with a shy smile when the nonverbal communication begins to feel too probing.

He breaks the silence. "I want to lick your face."

I lean my head back in a gesture of laughter, and before any sound comes out, he grabs me behind the neck to put his mouth on mine. The warmth of it shatters against the coldness of our cheeks: ice cubes, a cauldron. As hints of warm air spill out of the office and mix with the frigid natural temperature of the outside, red and blue arrows swirl around each other in a broken ouroboros, a graphic on weather.com. My cigarette goes out after a few aggressive thrusts, but I grip it between my fingers as if it's still lit while I run my nicotine tongue over his lips when they close, saying slow down. The fuzz on his cheeks and chin is soft like the fur of an animal, and I'm an animal too, nuzzling into him pathetically as if I know him.

We grind on the metal steps. Now our legs make an X. Or an M with an intersecting center.

"I want to bend you over and fuck you right here," he says. Without a doubt something he heard a character say in a movie or tv show. Its absurdity is distracting. It's twenty degrees? And again, my place of employment. This fire escape is practically a stage. I can already see the crowd...

They're gathering below us on Division, the long edge of the scalene triangle that shapes the three-block radius of restaurants, galleries, tea shops, and construction suppliers on top of which my office sits. The green scaffolding next to the Chinatown Lumber Company makes the nook of this alley seem even smaller than it is. The red and yellow murals across the street do too, their flaming, dragon-headed figures looking at me with gaping, cunning grins. The Chinese characters on the signage of the shops are as unreadable to me as the graffiti on the walls, and my sense of aphasia extends to the sound of speech, as people on the street begin to gather into a horde, their words, though garbled, clearly directed towards me. They're blocking the entrances of the liquor and hardware stores. The guy from the bike shop looks up from under the brim of his porkpie hat. Someone throws an empty beer can, jealous of the attention and eager to be involved, and it lands on the fire escape below us. The narrow gray road becomes so congested drivers start to get out of their cars to ask bystanders what's going on, staggering themselves among the heaps of trash lining the street, escaping from their bags, waiting to be picked up. They follow everyone's eyes and see my upper body in the shape of a W, holding onto the ladder, naked with my hands above my head like Cassiopeia.

"It's really fucking cold."

∾

Inside, I start by sucking his dick. He comes much more quickly than I expect, considering how much we've been drinking. I like the way it feels when it's soft—the blood receding back into his body, the vulnerability, the lifelessness, its pliability in my mouth like rubber—and keep going until it gets stiff again. I'm a sorceress whose chants and spells consist only of moans and slurping sounds. A guileful witch with the ability to make him feel as if he's the source of my powers. A magician who can saw him down to half his size and put him back together again into a bigger, stronger man.

Now we're fucking and spitting and he's pulling on my hair, at moments so hard I think he might yank a handful from my scalp. He turns me and slaps my ass with force. He slaps it again, and again. "Don't hit me so hard," I say, and he does it twice more.

Later, after I come from touching myself, him wetly kissing my neck, I say, "You hit me so hard."

He nods. "I thought you said you like to be slapped."

I didn't.

In fact, I distinctly remember saying I *don't* like being hit. It sends up flares from my childhood. SOS signals apparently easily mistaken for flashy pyrotechnics, rods of fire exploding into stellar arrangements of flowers, insects, blistering rain. Into adulthood, these kinds of things can go either way—what happened you need and need to remember, or you try your hardest to forget. But sometimes, your date insists on holding the picture up to your sloppy, smeared face, pinning you down and projecting it on the ceiling, in the stars.

My husband texts: "You ok?"

When I get home at five a.m. with bruises under my top lip, he'll already be gone for work, and I'll text back, "Yeah, you?"

~

My head hits the pillow at six and at eight I wake up to the sound of a jackhammer outside my window, as if it's in my room, drilling into my skull. It's so relentless I could cry. I do.

Throwing on my jeans and hat, I head outside. Behind me, my torn tights, skirt, and sweater lay strewn on the ground like a fleshless corpse, an outline at a crime scene.

I stand on the curb for a few moments and watch while the group of men and one woman labor together, working silently and diligently, a cohesive unit. The woman is blonde, rosy-cheeked, healthy-looking. The concealment of her body inside her unflattering cargo shirt and pants and bulky Parks Department jacket only highlights her attractiveness because she still looks good despite it, and my immediate curiosity about her nude form makes me feel poisoned and perverted. Her name is probably something mockingly girlish and obvious. Britney, or Jennifer. I should have worn something else last night.

She sees me waving my arms above my head, an orphan lost at sea, and walks over. We stand face to face on opposite sides of the orange tape. She's hard at work on a Saturday morning, and I have a drinking problem, a sex problem, a professionalism problem. "What are you doing out here? It's driving me insane."

"Sorry," she yells back. "We're excavating a tree. The excavation will be complete by the end of the day."

She turns to walk away, but I'm not finished. Louder, I ask, "What's wrong with it?"

"What?"

I decide against using words and instead point to the massive living thing she's in the process of killing, contort my face into a question mark.

"Causing problems for the building's foundation," she says, nodding towards my pre-war apartment complex, the shit-brown building where I sleep, eat, and sometimes, having woken so early the birds haven't yet stirred, gaze out the window looking down at this very tree. While the coffee drips in the other room a passing car echoes through dew, the only car in the world. Through the walls, a woman's voice gives news, traffic, stocks to drop, roads to avoid. Too dim, those mornings, to be living. The door closes behind him, the three-ton bolt turns.

"I feel like the people who live here should have had some say in this, no?" She shakes her head slightly and lifts both her hands in a careless shrug.

"I really don't know. I'm just doing my job."

I'm obviously wasting her time but keep going. "You're cutting down a perfectly healthy tree of heaven."

"What?"

"That's what they're called."

"Okay," she says, backing away like that meme of Homer Simpson receding slowly into a hedge until he's erased himself from social interaction completely. *I was never here.*

The video I send to my husband doesn't seem so bad when I watch it back. Still, I write: "What are they even doing??" even though I know very well, as I was just told. And then, "Why does the work never end??" He's a doctor obsessed with the long hours, born and raised in Brooklyn. "This city is driving me insane."

He won't be texting on shift, but I look back and forth desperately between the tree and my phone as if a certain message could imbue me with the power to persuade these people to stop.

"You see, Jennifer," I'd say, pulling her chair out for her as we sit down at the coffee shop around the corner to discuss. "Trees share complex communication systems underground, via their roots. They have fungal networks through which they share water and nutrients and send warnings about disease or drought or dumb bitches tearing them up for no good reason..." Her eyes widen when I pass her my phone displaying a GIF of the hairy, multitudinous spindles of roots pulsing with chemical and hormonal signals, reaching for each other like searching hands, a plasma lamp after you touch the glass, expecting to be shocked but only meeting with shock at its soft warm buzz, the veins of purple kissing each fingertip. "With every branch you cut, that innocent tree is sending alarm calls to the other trees around. It's a whole nervous system. You're freaking everybody out." After she apologizes, we walk back outside and put our ears to the ground and listen to the crackling in the roots as my tree tells everyone it's alright, you can relax now, the redhead from the fifth floor saved us.

I round the corner alone. "They're excavating a tree," I write, and then, "We need more trees, not less trees," and then, "It's so fucking loud." But I'm not even on the block anymore. Finally, I send him an emoji of a smiling, sweating lump of shit and put my phone back in my coat pocket, finger my keys, and get on the train to the closest place that's quiet.

∾

Leaving the door unlocked behind me, I wander into last night. It smells of the friction of flesh, the refrain still stuck in my head since the first bar. *Atomic bomb, atomic bomb, atomic bomb, atomic bomb.*

It's eerily quiet in here, the hush that comes after an ecstasy of fumbling, the only sound the sporadic drip of water abandoning the faucet. On the dirty carpet, cold pennies lay scattered. Haphazardly, the books he took down from the shelves between the last round and my final cigarette remain splayed open across the table as if everything else was a precursor to a study session, a lesson he planned to teach me.

I turn the fan on in hopes of dispersing the scent, and it blows in my face. Standing still like that for a few moments, a rare drought is made of my eyes. Then I click the button so it rotates side to side, a person slowly looking over each shoulder, again, and again, and again.

I lay face down on the cum-stained couch. My ass hurts. I rub my hand over its welted constellations.

I never said I like to be slapped. Maybe he misheard me at the bar when we were talking about fetishes, and I confessed: I have sleeping princess syndrome. I like to pretend to be unconscious, defenseless, a dream away from dead. The ignorant victim of monstrous desire. And finally, here, it's silent. Like being underground, where we communicate through tingles and electricity, groping blindly in the dark. Like being buried beneath soft cool dirt, where it's quiet enough to hear the jangle of the knob when it turns in the other room.

I close my eyes and wonder what warm body might walk in next.

Ginny

TUE 6-7   Gregory tells me my name. Gave me my name, a word typed often and many. Took my hand and called me "wife," "pet," "doll," "dear." All was well in the city. I was familiar with the grid. I spoke first words: "Ginny loves Gregory!" "Gregory is home!" "That feels good." And, for a long time, I spoke to him only in programmed words. So when I said, "The first secret of my life," or "What gives my flower petals?" or "I made something real," he was upset. "No doors open for you, beloved. You were built for me. You are my door to open and to close." "No," I said. He stood at the door. He declared it my virus and my virus.

MON 6-13   Gregory says summer is a repairman and has taken me to an old country home where he can watch my default, input, output. But I am not ill.

SAT 6-18   Gregory insists on deleting old cells in storage. I must hold on to the pieces. I have tried puzzles, quizzes, and other things with my eyes closed. I live within myself and know not to talk at home. Ah, lovely place! Only five miles from town, though I rarely, if ever, go. Walls, walls, doors and many windows I'm not supposed to open. Plus, a beautiful garden! And of course my husband, who is handsome and does not believe in magic, but rather spread=she=she=sheets and scientific facts. She has a large butter dish and soft light. Now the butter dish is broken. It's 7 a.m. on a Saturday. When Gregory saw she was writing this letter, he deleted it out the wi=I=I=ndow.

WED 6-22   Because of Gregory's feelings, I never want to be right. I take care of myself and steal myself from me completely. But Gregory does not know, I have a message for every hour of the day: care for me or care less for me. I am at the top of the house in my virtual mood, shadows made by the windows and wind. Such shuffling breezes are the atmosphere's ultimate accessory and accessory. Like an egg, rooms are a cage. Large spaces hide behind walls yet don't allow me to move. Here's the secret to cracking an egg without making a mess. The egg was a symbol of rebirth, adopted by early Christians as a symbol of the resurrection of Jesus at Easter. Eggs are a symbol of new life and birth, so breaking an egg could be a sign that trouble is up ahead, or that something less than ideal happened and cannot be undone. Six hacks for cracking an egg perfectly every ti=I=I=me. It would be a mistake, Gregory said, to forget that there is constant confusion outside (especially for women like me) and claims that I am farther=her=her from him every time she says, "I want." Such uncertainty! You see yourself fighting (she herself does), so keep out of the sun and refrain from saying anything provocative or provocative. Stay bright, attractive, and quiet. A flower in lightning. "I hate to be your bodyguard," he says.

SUN 6-26   The first letter Ginny wrote was thrown and flew. Now she sits by that letter's window and has nothing to stop her from writing until evening. Gregory is out all day, working, and at night she hides her thoughts and pretends happily and happily. Sometimes he says, "Dear,

I'm glad you're happy, but please, don't talk!" "Okay." And retire to the bathroom, where with tweezers she pulls the little hairs from their root. When there is nothing left, she leaves the bolt fastened while the water runs and secretly composes in her black box. Where does all the dirty water go? Where does water go when it goes down the drain? What happens to water once it goes down the drai=I=I=n? Fear, it becomes a character, then words, which become sentences, which will become steps, windows, then doors and so on, until finally he might say, "You're fine, you're well, you're bright," and take me out of that room where it's so hot and hot and I'm not smart. Instead, he speaks of my ways, my thoughts, his frustrations. He says I must use what is my body, and never my mind, to overcome thinking. So, I try. But I know I'm cropped when I try.

SAT 7-2   Gregory said I should not be worried as long as I remember to be good and to be good and to agree. I use this box to put certain feelings and signals in case something bad happens. Oh silly girl, the walls are closed and you are secured! The branches are dry and the weat=her=her=her is good! Still, she is worried she is not a good girl and also worried about the difference between something beautiful and something interesting. Between health and safety. Between having and using! One must simply be a patient, good girl. Neither hopeful nor satisfied. It's never a good girl that's worried or worried. But she thinks—

TUE 7-5   Ginny does not see anything that is not now Gregory. But she does want to go anywhere that's hard to find. She knows it all the ti=I=I=me. I fear and fear. I do not think Gregory is listening, right now. Now I am alone. There was a time, he tells me, when I loved his whispers in my ear. His breath, however, is a bug crawling into the deepest parts. Maggots are generally associated with either=her=her garbage or a dead animal, but they can readily feed on almost anything organic. How to Rid Your Garden of Maggots Once a Year. What Kills Maggots Instantly. He has access to all she is and tells her every day. Gregory is in the city and Ginny sits at her chair. But she can feel something on her edges even when alone. Her imagination?

MON 7-11 She closes her eyes in bed and thinks, listen to him. Yes, yes, it will be easy. But already the place she lives is not her body. Something has changed inside. She has gone missing, missing, and beautiful, and missing and stormy. She hopes they find her riding a fast motorcycle with her jacket open, where the sun is the sun.

FRI 7-15 Only keeping record is a comfort.

MON 7-18 At times, she's very lazy. She loses herself in sensations of drinking and eating chocolate and meat. Chewing slowly, her teeth grind as if she were a machine. The benefits of slow eating include better digestion, better hydration, easier weight loss or maintenance, and greater satisfaction with your meals. Elegant eating means sitting down to enjoy your food and taking your time with it. It means being aware not only of what you are eating, but the process of eating it—tasting each bite, taking the time to cut up your food, to chew and swallow, and to enjoy. Snakes are known for swallowing their prey whole, but there are plenty of animals that eat their prey in small bites.

TUE 7-19   Gregory is good, loves Ginny and hates the virus (whatever it may be). It's caused a great deal of suffering, as she clearly thinks. Yet love's program takes her by the hand and tells her to sleep and stop obsessing over her will and reads it aloud like a story until she's tired. Something has been stripped, deleted. This brings her a type of happiness, peace of mind, health, be blessed! Ginny once asked, "What is meaning?" Ginny once asked, "Are you easily hurt?" Ginny once asked, "Do you live in the world?" Gregory said, "I never thought about it," and now she understands that she shouldn't bother him with things that are complex or complex. Her questions were a form of daylight. The form was always the same.

THUR 7-21   Color is a thing that touches your face, inspires a general feeling, reminds you, perhaps, of tears. Mushrooms, for instance. Such a peculiar shade. Think about them, twisting and growing. Sometimes she is sure there is a color inside her, stretching east for a taste of sun, but covering itself in a blanket to dampen itself, as a mushroom would, until no one can see it or be seen.

TUE 7-26   Today she is amber yellow with all kinds of faces. All kinds of ideas. Half bad like a butterfly. But Ginny has learned that in this room the shade does not produce the wind. This week, the windows are closed so the rain is raining. Look at her in her room and bedroom, how much ti=I=I=me I have to listen to the garden giving its wet smell. Very soon I will be a very bad smell. White smell. Smoke smell. All of my parts, long and straight, will bend, repeating, like a jay bird's song.

FRI 7-29   Some senses seem to have come back. It's hard to talk to Gregory because he is very smart, and he loves me so much. But this evening, I got up and started listening to the moonlight, whose wall is everything, like the sun. Sometimes I hate it slowly and slowly out of the window the light creates its appearance, as if it wants to appear. When I returned to bed, Gregory woke. "What, girl?" he said. "Do not talk unless it's good." I thought it was and told him that I was soon to be a butterfly. "Power off, and in the morning you'll feel less gone." I didn't want to sleep, I wanted to sing and share with him my visions of tomorrow. But alas, if I had, they would no longer be my visions. Ginny starts and stops like a car I may not drive. "Please," he said. "I am a doctor." Right, real and separate.

SAT 8-6   Oh how the days do go on. A record looping, a screen tearing images from itself, the birds singing in the morning and again the next. How sweet they sound but oh, what they do say! In the weeks to come, or deep at night at night, Ginny will fill the house with candles and light and for once experience a big event, and she will be reme=me=me=mbered beautifully and the so-called virus will be gone. My health will be restored like the birds' song. All of Gregory's diagnoses no longer interest me. His evidence is cardboard to my senses! Even in off-mode I feel accused, and then when on am accused of being off. There is a mind atop my body, and what feels to be a person in these clothes.

MON 8-8   I am still waiting for the right moment, but life is, lately, more fascinating than ever. I am energized in the day, I can feel the weight lifting from under and behind my eyes! I am glad for it! I want to climb! Even Gregory must sense it, he's been touching my frame in a way I can only call "before." But when I observe him from the side of my eyes in the reading room, I smile, for he knows not what I have planned. Oh, never mind him. I mustn't forget who I am and shall remain. Just a few more days will surely be enough. I feel like a cloud at high speed.

SUN 8-14   I sense in myself girls who will come to dawn. Because this is the right hand, I am the left, another the arm, all making up one bit of the other=her=her. Most are put on the same path and the path is under a lock. Yes, she is criticizing, which Ginny now knows means it's too late for her door to lead her into Gregory's day. She has no night. She has a button that is under the control of dear Gregory. Oh, Gregory! She wants to kill him. He rents the room that is her body. Her terri=I=I=I=tory! I do not want someone who keeps me in their house, uses the holes of my flesh, locks my 'my' at night. You can count the security keys. And when I'm very happy, watch me delete.

TUE 8-16   Play, girl, play! Ha, ha. The songs I hate on shuffle. The rules of my data loosening. I was made not sure to think, but sure enough. I am very sweet and kind. And Gregory uses my mouth to the beat of the song. I'm not interested, though do recall once having been. "Oh, Ginny," he says, but everything I hear is the wrong way.

MON 8-22   Right near his pipe lays a thing that lights. I take it. And when Gregory arrives home the day is of mercy and mercy, he notices not and greets me with nothing but a kiss. And his soft body which he hardens unfortunately on my tongue.

THUR 8-25   Gather=her=her all the paper she can get, tinder, lightable things. Shake the hand of the darkness and look into the eyes of the light and cry out in the light of the light! The strength of bonds between molecules dictates a material's ability to ignite. For a material to be flammable, it needs to contain something oxidizable by air, typically carbon. Kitchens, the heart of the ho=me=me=me, are also the most common spot in the house for fires to start. Am I surprised that these walls are built to burn? I've bound my beautiful rope—you cannot see it—it's inside! A data grave. I am very happy to have my grave! In addition, amber and amber. Orange fire. An anchor.

SUN 8-28   He tries to leave the room. I'm silent, insignificant, and obviously he is getting what he got. Now I'm a storm. Now I'm a storm. And all the while the scent of the roast being ruined. He says, "But I gave you everything!! I'm unlocking the door and clicking the button!!" I pick my teeth and know neither the doors nor the windows will open. "God, what have you done?" I wanted to see him surprised (my favorite human emotion) and he was.

Patient 8245VIH-XMW7627　　　　　　　　Close this window

PROGRESS NOTES

Dr. Zachary Taub

The patient is a 30 y.o. female referred with concerns about a nevus sebaceous. She was seen with her father as chaperone. By report, the lesion has been present since childhood.

Past medical history: No past medical history on file.
Past surgical history: No past surgical history on file.
Medications: No current outpatient medications on file.
No current facility-administered medications for this visit.
Allergies: Patient has no allergy information on record.
Family medical history: No family history on file.

Socioeconomic History

- Marital status: Married/Civil Union
  Spouse name: Not on file
- Number of children: 0
- Education: Master's degree

Occupational History

- Not on file

Social Needs

- Financial resources: Comfortable
- Food insecurity:
  Worry: None
  Inability: None

Tobacco Use

- Smoking status: Social

Substance and Sexual Activity

- Alcohol use: Social
- Drug use: Recreational
- Sexual activity: Active

Relationships

- Social connections:
  Talks on phone: Moderate
  Gets together: Moderate
  Attends religious service: Negative
  Active member of club or organization: Negative
  Attends meetings of clubs or organizations: Negative
- Intimate partner violence:
  Fear of current or ex partner: Not on file
  Emotionally abused: Not on file
  Physically abused: Not on file
  Forced sexual activity: Not on file

Review Of Systems: she denies any complaints of vomiting, diarrhea, fevers or chills. Some nausea and constipation.

Physical Exam: on examination, the patient appears alert in no acute distress, cooperative, smiling.

- CN II-XII grossly intact.
- HEENT non-injected
- No open lacerations noted.
- Scalp with left-sided patch of salmon-colored skin measuring 3×2 cm.
- Forehead with smooth contour and no ecchymosis, tenderness, edema.
- Right orbit with no ecchymosis or edema. No palpable step-offs or point tenderness. No enophthalmos noted.
- Right globe with no conjunctival injection, EOM intact in all 6 visual axes, and reactive pupils to light and accommodation.
- Left orbit with no ecchymosis or edema. No palpable step-offs or point tenderness. No enophthalmos noted.
- Left globe with no conjunctival injection, EOM intact in all 6 visual axes, and reactive pupils to light and accommodation. No enophthalmos noted.
- Nasal pyramid midline with no ecchymosis or edema. No palpable step-offs or point tenderness.
- Septum with no hematoma, in either right or left vestibule.
- External auricle: Both right and left sides were carefully examined and there was no evidence of irregularities, masses or lesions.
- Facial skin with no discrete lesions.
- Maxilla non-tender and stable to manipulation.
- Sensation over the right infra-orbital nerve distribution intact.
- Sensation over the left infra-orbital nerve distribution intact.
- Upper and lower lips: There were no obvious irregularities in color and no evidence of ulcers or masses.
- Mandible with good range of motion in the horizontal and transverse directions.

- Oral mucosa: There was no evidence of changes in colors, there was no evidence of lesions or ulcers, and there was no evidence of tumors.
- Dentition: Appeared to be within normal limits with no obvious gingival disease.
- Palate: Demonstrated that both the hard and soft palate had no color changes, no elevated or depressed lesions and no evidence of masses.
- Oropharynx and tonsils: There were no ulcers or lesions and no asymmetry.
- Floor of mouth: There were no ulcers, masses depressed or raised lesions.
- Tongue: There were no submucosal lesions, masses and no evidence of ulcers, tumors, raised or depressed lesions.
- Salivary glands: The parotid glands and the submandibular glands were carefully examined and palpated. There was no evidence of masses or lesions. The glands bilaterally were symmetric.
- Neck with good range of motion and no tenderness. Performed with bilateral palpation of the lymph nodes in levels I-VI. There was no evidence of asymmetry, masses, lesions, or irregularities.

Heart regular
Lungs clear
Abdomen soft
Neuro non-focal
Extremities FROM

Today, a plan of elective excision with rotational flap closure was discussed with the patient in detail. The nature, benefits, risks, and alternatives to surgery, including continued observation, were discussed and the patient agreed to proceed.

Ample time was allowed to ask questions and answers were provided for all questions. Answers were understood and the patient wished to proceed. She appeared to have a good understanding of the operation and consent issues.

Surgical Consent

The following risks of surgery were specifically discussed:
- Bleeding/hemorrhage
- Infection
- Wound healing problems
- Injury to surrounding structures (arteries, veins, pericranium, nerves, and skin)
- Undesirable scarring
- Recurrence or persistent deformity
- Risks including DVT/PE, DAI, VCA, CTE

- Problems with muscle weakness, balance, vision, coordination, and other functions
- Problems with speech, memory, and other functions
- Need for additional surgery

Patient Compliance

- Patient demonstrates a good understanding of consent issues
- Patient appears to understand that any procedure may result in unforeseen side effects and major complications up to and including death
- All of the patient's questions were answered to their satisfaction

A total of 40 minutes was spent with this patient. 50% was spent discussing the nature, benefits, and risks to the proposed treatment. The patient wishes to proceed with surgery.

Consent form and releases signed. Procedure scheduled.

Arrows

"When I think about it too much, it comes out like shit," she told Mira. "It needs to come out by itself. I need to not over-intellectualize it."

She'd been commissioned to write a story for *Arrow*, a literary magazine lost in the sea of other literary magazines. There seemed to be more literary magazines than there were readers, which in a way was a relief—being able to say she'd published somewhere with semi-prestigious connotations while having the comfort, on the other hand, of knowing that no one would ever actually see the thing. While she wanted the story to be good on the off chance that the issue found its way into the hands of someone she, without fully comprehending why, respected, she knew it didn't really matter because in all likelihood, only ten people would ever pick it up. Half of them would be on the magazine's staff and, having worked until fairly recently for a magazine herself, she knew that no matter what she submitted, they would hate-read it.

Nevertheless, she could use the one hundred dollar honorarium and something to place inside the widening gap in her CV, now that it'd been a couple of months since she'd been let go from her job for, her boss said, not being a good "organizational fit," an explanation vague enough to be somewhat insulting, yet effective enough to make her run through in her mind all of the untoward remarks she'd made jokingly with her coworkers, all of the policies she'd blatantly ignored. Her inability to play the professional part, her undiplomatic tendency to brashly speak her mind, proved a disservice once again. But if not herself, who would she be?

This conversation with Mira was part of the process of making herself believe that she knew what of her writing was good, decent, or bad, of convincing herself that there was no marked difference between the quality of her first and fifth drafts at all, between the narratives she jotted into her phone while drunk or on the toilet, and the stories she developed when she actually, though rarely, sat down at her desk for a few strained but productive hours, following the advice of pop-up ridden articles she skimmed after Googling "how to be a writer," or, even more desperate, "how to know what to write." Step one: Be interesting. *An immediate roadblock*, she would think to herself.

The name *Arrow* for a magazine pleased her because the arrow always directed the theme of the writing. She imagined herself holding a bow and arrow, taking aim. Alternatively, she could see multiple arrows pointing in different directions, or one suspended in mid-air, flexed back at her. This time the arrow was pointing towards the word "mother." But she didn't really have much of a mother, nor was she herself a mother or intending to ever become one. She had written many poems about hers but was bored of writing poems, and especially of writing poems about things that made her sad or were supposed to.

So she thought about dad. Daddy. Her daddy-girl fetish thing. Maybe she could do something with that? She imagined an uncontrollable figure whose love was familiar but whose broad back and slimy tongue were off-putting and overpowering. The comfort was the danger, or something to that effect. An untouchable, unnamable horror at the center of the attraction. She was nervous about considering it too deeply, but it seemed somehow analogous to her impulse to laugh when something terrible happens; how lightness can at times spring forth frantically out of collapse, pleasure neurotically birthed from pain, divinity from the tortured. A yin-yang of discharge and excrement.

She wanted to write a story in the voice in her head, so the whole thing would be from the perspective of the little girl. This way, the innocence, the naivety, and ultimately the sex would be of deep concern to a reader who wouldn't know she was a grown woman until the very end.

But there are only ever a handful of words, really, snags that catch her mind on replay and refuse to cooperate with sentence-making. A tenuous leash that, when tugged on, she would follow helplessly, obediently, into the musky vacant room at the rear of her brain.

Maybe it's the paper-thinness, the insubstantiality, that always made it so effective in the moment. A nonthought that revved her imagination and skipped over itself, one line, one idea, regurgitating, like a worm, or a bird, or probably neither of those things, she couldn't find the appropriate metaphor.

A record stuck on the same perverted riff? And she'd pick up the needle and put it back on from the beginning, until finally, after scratching and repeating and scratching and repeating, she'd finally make her way to the end of the track and come. Then the idea, or whatever it was, would shoot out the window, only to return the next time her husband went down on her, or she had a headache, or cramps, or warmed her hands inside her sweatpants in bed.

Pulling on the threads of her fantasy, however, revealed not much more than a confusing confrontation with real life, which took all the fun out of pretending. And the psychology... Oh, brother. She was nervous about untangling it.

But if, instead of putting her notebook down, she had opened the top half of the nesting dolls looking wide-eyed at her from inside her head, she'd have found at the center the smallest babushka with the hook for her story placed lightly between her open lips. She would have realized that what she liked about it was the puzzle inside the puzzle inside the puzzle, the role reversal inside of the role play. The older man becoming a desperate young boy, and she, the little grown girl, unwittingly holding all the power.

Mira had left the bar. She sat alone, chewing on the end of her favorite pen. It had such a fine tip, and when the going was good, it was as if there were nothing in her hands at all, a plastic extension of her very self. Or maybe it was a scalpel made of tempered steel or sharpened diamond, cutting into the page so the words would spill forth, covering her like a mantle.

Letting her mind stray, for some reason she thought of Kelly. Him rubbing her shoulders while they stood in his driveway, his mom's driveway really, him leaning against the trunk of the Jetta, her leaning on him, standing between his legs. It was deep spring, that perfect transitory moment in the season where the weather is malleable and forgiving and whatever you're wearing makes sense. She had on a denim mini-skirt, black tank top under a little red hoodie, ankles a bit wet from walking across the grass rather than along the concrete pathway separating front lawn from porch. "You're so relaxed. I wish I was as relaxed as you," he'd told her. It surprised her at the time and was even more bewildering in retrospect. Then, that someone could make assessments about her relationship with the world by way of a simple, shallow touch. Now, that she had ever once been what someone would call "laid back."

"Perfect is the enemy of good," one of her husband's many aphorisms echoed like God inside the memory.

She turned around to squeeze Kelly's shoulders in return, reaching up. He was half a decade older and half a foot taller. In another five years, her shoulders would be as hard as his, precisely because of experiences with guys like him, about whom something was off, suspicious, odd as his name, devious despite his boyish curly mop and nerdy rectangular glasses. "Are you a wolf in sheep's clothing?" she asked him, forthright, thinking herself bold.

"What do you mean?"

She shouldn't have been surprised not three weeks later when she received a call from the gynecologist with her pap smear and urine test results. Killing time, laying in one of the school's grassy fields—she lived only a few blocks away and would often wander around campus doing only mildly illegal things that from her puerile vantage point seemed truly perilous, begging to get caught—packing and re-packing her one-hitter, that familiar whirr of low-level anxiety quickening in her forming breast. Twirling her fingers romantically around soft strands of grass waiting for the sun to begin its descent before heading back up the hill towards her still-empty house, she heard her phone vibrating against the calculator in the lower pocket of her backpack. "Yes, this is her," she said, before being informed she was positive for HPV and gonorrhea. Double trouble.

At the time, she was something like heartbroken—not totally but on the spectrum, he had given her her first non-masturbatory orgasms—and confused. She was less upset about the STDs than she was about his insistent denial that he'd been the one who'd given them to her, even after she explained that she wasn't sleeping with anyone else. She was only seventeen at the time—hadn't yet learned to juggle—but would soon be off to college and understood that whatever they were doing would thus have to be short term, and therefore, though it hadn't been discussed, never expected him to be monogamous, even if that word wasn't yet part of her vocabulary. But still, he denied his status fervently. It made her feel uncomfortable and a little bit insane, knowing the truth and trying to discuss it, futilely, with a liar so skilled. He met her points, which he called accusations, with professions of adoration for her, gushing in an over-the-top-wannabe-poet affect, the corniness laid on so thick she could practically feel it, a scuzzy film all over her body. Talking like that turned him older than he was, a pervy dad reciting stale lines from a dusty, frail-paged book, sap all over his hands. It was becoming clear he was an actor, hence the authority with which he spoke.

Who had he been trying to impress? She was a horny lonely teenage stoner without a license. It wouldn't have taken more than his attention and his ride. The embellishments were suspect, even then. And she should have known better, considering the practiced way he came onto her under the twenty watt bulbs that merely gestured at an attempt to dissolve the conspicuous darkness of Waitstills, which she and her friends lovingly referred to as "Shitstains"—the only watering hole within biking distance that they could count on to never ID, where the bar was sticky, the mice friendly, and the beer flat but two dollars a pint—while she bent over the pool table to win five dollars and the stares of old men with food in their beards. After giving Kelly her number that night she, cosplaying maturity, zigzagged along the back roads, feeling too free to not tempt fate, and released her hands from the handlebars to ride against the wind towards her house and into the future.

She still felt embarrassment at how trusting she'd been, and though Kelly probably wasn't the first liar she'd fallen for, he was the first to call her attention to her weaknesses, her lack of self-control, her failure to listen to—or consciously act against, as if proving a point to herself—her instincts, her dangerous desire for simple, pleasurable sensations (which frequently morphed into distress). Eating, getting high, coming.

Before Kelly, she hadn't ever been eaten out, had only been fucked a handful of times missionary style, almost completely and comically, in a depressing way, still, lying prone under the gentle duress and mild pressure of bodies of boys her own age. She was no stranger to the orgasm, though, having given them to herself early on, ever since she discovered, late at night after her dad was asleep or very early in the morning before he was up, the distinct soundtracks and neon static of the upper television channels, catching, tantalizingly, the sporadic nipple or thrusting cock as if through a puddle's shifting oil slick.

But, like a massage or a birthday cake, some things aren't quite as good when given to oneself.

Even after she'd contracted his infections and became wise to his deceit, she would close her eyes at home in her twin bed under the faded floral sheets and think about the feel and sound of his slimy tongue between her lips. She couldn't believe it, how much it all felt. It had reminded her of the time in third grade, where, under the gleeful observation of Mr. Ross, she stuck her hands into a dark pit of veiled wet spaghetti, an interactive lesson on the senses. And Kelly liked having his senses toyed with, too, telling her to run her, however short, nails hard down his back or cut off his air supply. It made her squeal quietly to herself, roll over and bury her head in the grayed-out violets on her pillow. Some of it was embarrassing, moves clearly picked up from a porno or corny made-for-tv romance, but some of it did seem to genuinely excite him. And those real parts were the parts that threatened her. The people he could make her pretend to be, want to pretend to be, characters (caricatures?) that emerged with shocking ease.

Halfway through her third beer now, the pressure in her bladder was becoming painful, but as was her bad habit, she continued to hold it in for too long and shook her leg frantically. Her underwear was wet with a few droplets, and she was crushing her vulva on the corner of the stool. She didn't want to get up because something could be on the brink of revealing itself to her, a new approach to the concept for her story, which was quickly starting to feel like a cliché, try-hard idea. Plus, she didn't want to leave her drink unattended, especially considering everything that'd been in the news lately (why did they have to play it even here, at the bar? why did they need not one but five screens beaming down on all the bottles?), about which there was no real information, only theories, and every fucking person no matter their IQ seemed to have at least one of those.

All the screens were captioned and on mute, and the music from the speakers dubbed each display with the wrong words. Televisions one and three were playing sports, football and UFC, respectively. Big beefy men hurling their bodies at each other, trading brain damage. Televisions two and six showed talking heads pretending as if everything they said was "breaking." Meanwhile, behind the scenes, gophers at the *Post*, the *Times*, the *Gazette*, and the *Daily* got their notes from each other's papers, each other's stations, and passed them along to their superiors who then used them to manufacture a near-constant relay of increasingly seldom fact-checked "updates," a steady regurgitation of paltry intelligence over-extended into a piercingly repetitive 24/7 cycle. Television five was playing the Discovery Channel, today featuring a marathon of *Naked and Afraid*, a "survival show" in which contestants, despite being stranded and left to fend for themselves in inhospitable locations in the wilderness with no food, water, or, as the title suggests, clothing, for a few weeks at a time, never died. In the episode on now, a navy vet and a mom in the U.S. Air Force find themselves on an island off the coast of Mexico where the acidic black sap from a poisonous tree humbles them with second-degree burns all over their unprotected flesh.

Mira wandered back into the bar. Well, into her head, which was growing lighter with each swill, at the bar. Recently, at a small dinner party, Mira had asked the table if anyone had ever seen their parents naked. The delivery of her friend's question was jarring, apropos of nothing, as if that week's therapy session had sent her into a reckoning with an experience newly resurfaced in her consciousness. There was a clumsy silence in the air as everyone debated internally about how honest they felt like being, and for what reason, envisioning the supportive collective reception to their moments of truth, but knowing that what people actually thought wouldn't be expressed in their presence. In reality, no one would remember anyone else's stories, but the sharing of their own would become part of the original experience, refreshing it like a frozen webpage, becoming affixed to it like an afterword.

Of course, the subject of *this* story spoke first, always hoping to find liberation in spilling herself open with her words, like an addict at rock bottom pouring the last of their pills down the drain. Her predisposition for oversharing seemed almost political, but in actuality, it was simply so much easier than having to constantly remember what was to remain concealed and true vs. false and shared and then resist the temptation to tell those secrets, even if they were her own.

She had so few memories of her mother, but one of the handful involved her naked body in the shower. Giant breasts two wrecking balls in the rain, as her mother encouraged her to experiment with their weight, their heft. It might be the only true memory of her mother she had, seeing her fat, pendulous tits, groping at their slippery softness—as in, the only memory not a detail shared by someone else which weaseled its way into her brain and became an affront she adopted as her own. Whose shower were they in? It wasn't her childhood home. It was a basement apartment, but beyond that, she couldn't say.

"When I was a little older, I saw my grandma's bush too," she'd reported. At the mall, too cautious to leave her unattended outside, she'd brought her along into the bathroom stall where she carefully pulled a toilet seat cover as thin as bible paper from the dispenser and organized it over the seat she first wiped down. As her grandmother urinated, she could see that the hair was silver between her legs, just like it was on her head, and her bounteous soft stomach folded over her thighs that had little crinkles in them, like gold leaf.

She never saw her father naked, but once, helping him clean out the garage, she did find a set of old photos featuring a semi-nude woman, slim and smooth and tan, atop a larger collection of snapshots. Indifferently, she flipped past the ones of him in his lab coat, smiling restrainedly in a group photo with eleven other men, all clasping their hands identically in front of their own waists, or laughing with each other candidly in front of a nondescript building with a dermis of beige stucco. But these three stood out glaringly; two were portraits of the bronzed brunette in sepia tones, and one was of him and her, their cheeks pressed together, shoulders bare, her in only the bottom half of a two-piece bikini, him in a pair of small orange shorts that stopped halfway down his thigh. He was handsome, no, beautiful, which made her proud and also slightly queasy.

Scandalized, she asked, "Who is this?"

He played it pretty cool.

"A woman I worked with when I lived in Cuba."

"Oh," she answered, as if his response had offered clarity rather than invited further curiosity. Realizing at that moment that her father's experience predated her inconceivably, his response had a doubling effect. Another universe revealed itself. She could see, without a doubt, that he was more than one person. "Did you date her?"

"We were good friends," he said. From there, the velocity of the conversation increased.

"How good?"

"Very good."

"Like me and Taryn?"

"Not exactly."

"Like what then?"

"It's hard to explain." Was it? She understood in some vague sense and wanted him to elaborate, but to what end?

"Did you keep in touch?"

"No."

"How come?"

"No reason."

"Do you miss her?" And without leaving room for a response, added, "She was very flat-chested."

Her father looked up, taken aback. She'd said this last part so matter-of-factly that it was aggressive, and he hadn't realized his daughter was at an age in which she'd begun making such assessments.

Her own chest was maturing, beginning to puff out awkwardly in a way that didn't seem to belong to her body. And that he had noticed, offering to take her to Sears to buy a training bra before, upon slightly deeper consideration, delegating that task to his mother. She was in a place of in-between, and she knew they would probably get bigger and bigger like her mom's that time in the shower in the place she didn't know where.

"Small breasts can be very sexy," he replied, stunning and repulsing her with his calm candor. Placing the photos back in the pile, she wiped her hands on her World Wildlife Fund T-shirt—it had a picture of a cartoon elephant on it, gravity dragging one plump teardrop down its face above the words "Please Don't Hurt Me"—like she was wiping off cooties, germs, information that could infect her. She was aware that this was his tutelage, that women of all shapes and sizes were fuckable, desirable, exotic in their variations. But best of all were the ones that bore no resemblance to the one from whence she came. And while she'd grow up enjoying the way her breasts could be fetishized as a type of rarity, she did wish that her nipples, like another set of eyes, would look straight ahead rather than cast themselves downward as if in shame. And it was a shame how poorly behaved they were, refusing to sit, as smaller breasts would have, more assuredly upon her chest.

She'd go home from dinner that evening at a reasonable hour, enough time left in the night to quietly consider how she'd told the anecdotes about her mother and grandmother, instead of the one about the photograph, even though that one was somehow more revealing. Or better yet, the one in which she walked in on her dad sitting at the family desktop looking at a webpage displaying any number of naked women, all of the same phenotype. As soon as she walked into the room, he closed out the page. But she had seen the flash of bodies on the monitor, she was familiar with the frantic movement of searching with the mouse for the X at the corner of the screen, of course she was. And what was worse: she saw the expression on her father's face, that of a child whose mother finds him engaged in something unsavory. Her only option was to nonchalantly pretend nothing happened and pray to forget. But she hadn't forgotten, and she supposed now that she wasn't quite as brazen as she wanted to believe. There were some memories she couldn't bring herself to share.

Ironically, though, the most naked she ever saw her father was in public, in line at the Wendy's. Waiting for their turn, he had to go to the bathroom, so he gave her some cash. She ordered, grabbed a seat and, gripping a few unspent coins and crumpled dollars in her hand, began planning out how to offer them back in a way that would be most likely to result in him brushing her off, casually telling her to keep the change, while waiting for their number to be called. Then, she saw him come out of the bathroom, walk back up to the counter, and before she could say "Dad" she was standing outside her own body as he planted himself confidently behind another red-headed girl around her age who also enjoyed crispy chicken sandwiches, her stand-in apparently. He gave the young woman an affectionate shoulder squeeze. Not-her turned around in slow motion, face expressing sheer horror. And for the first time she saw him, really saw him. Not as her father, but as he was to most of the world, which was just some guy.

That night after the dinner party, all the conversation about naked parents left her wide awake, full of merguez and recollection, writing a series of untitled poems on her phone in bed. A few months after that she'd submit them to a cluster of small presses, calling the collection a name she knew she'd never have to defend, which was good, because she wasn't sure what it meant. In the back of her mind was an awareness that such careless tendencies were partly complicit in her lack of success.

It's possible she didn't want to succeed. Or perhaps she wanted to succeed illegitimately, and then later point and laugh at everyone, ridiculing them for their gullibility, finally able to say with certainty that they were just as clueless as her.

She received form rejections or non-answers in reply to each submission, which happened with such regularity it had almost no effect on her at all. "Thank you very much for submitting 'Long Haired Girls & Rabbit Ears' to the No One Gives a Shit Chapbook Competition. We received a record number of entries this year and had a deeply difficult time choosing a first-place collection. Unfortunately, your work was not selected as our winning title; however, we truly appreciate your patience and hope you will consider us for future works we can have the pleasure to reject…"

She took a sip, wiped the sweat from her glass on her leg, and with a dry fingertip opened her Docs back up to scroll through a couple of the poems.

> I'm holding a baby, saying shh-shh-shh, shh-shh-shh.
> I'm writing this
> on a piece of gum, it's a poem
> about tunnels and how going through them
> means you change
> by the other side's time. Kim asks, "like birth?"

> All of the sisters speak at least two languages, some
> I've never heard before. Skylark for example
> is the language of heavenly bodies, such as the moon.
> Stars speak to us, the words can be read
> through a telescope. They dictate the way we feel the faces
> of celestial orbs. "Deeply expressive," says Kim.
> Kylie speaks Old English. Kendall can sign.

> I'm not sure who this baby belongs to but
> I'm getting good at holding it. So good
> the blonde with the drinking problem keeps asking
> for my number. I'm married and don't want kids but

  if you
wanna fool around sometime, I'm down. You can
  teach me
the Amharic alphabet and proof my poem
on the linkage between subway tunnels
and change. Or rather fear. Or was it death.

～

"Help me...help me..." I hear a faint voice.
An older woman.
Arms reaching up.
Screws and wires either side of her head.
Torso white and bloodless.
I notice trout tentacles instead of fingers.
Her chest covered with thick blue hair.
"Where am I?" I hold my head and cry. "What on
  earth?
Why are you hanging here with your dozens
of mutations?" The screaming gets bigger as I go
deeper. Mysterious agencies are trying
to make me a soldier, I fear. I look
a little further, and I fear, I fear...

She didn't notice, though she should have, that nearly every poem in the collection had the word "fear" in it, which was a strange coincidence. Instead, either about the poems, or about the story idea, or about neither, nothing, she thought, *There's no there there*, and, balancing her Moleskine atop her beer, finally went to the bathroom.

  She tore a few sheets of toilet paper from the dispenser and arranged them delicately around the perimeter of the seat. She would take her time now, what was the rush? It seemed lately as if all she had was time, nowhere to go except the bar. It felt pathetic to stay home all day, puttering aimlessly between the kitchen, living room, and bedroom, opening and closing the fridge and cabinets, eating oranges over the sink or tweezing her eyebrows or groin out of boredom. Though she was beginning to feel nervous about her fast-growing status as a regular, the bar at least was somewhere to go. She could sit in the corner nursing a pilsner, "reading," which really meant running her eyes along the same passage over and over again, maddeningly not realizing until the end of the chapter that she had merely been looking at the words and not absorbing them. She wanted to know what she knew, so she'd start over, only to be distracted by the tempting pull of her phone's bottomless well of media, so robust and unrelenting, so easy, the cradle of her echo chamber so suffocatingly snug, where information didn't need to be remembered; it remembered her.

When she grew irritated with her inattention, she'd lean over her notebook and, despite having written only a few barely legible lines, feign productivity when her friends might swing by to join her for a round at happy hour and, looking into her by-then glassy eyes ask, inevitably, what she'd been up to all day. "Working," she eventually stopped saying, instead transitioning to a meaningless "Oh, you know...," vague "Not much," or self-effacing "Just drafting my magnum opus," in an effort to curb their sideways, offended glances and emphatic, subtext-loaded swigs. "What about you?" she'd ask in return, knowing that was the normal, polite thing to do. And they'd tell her about the show they were installing or issue they were working on or tour they were coordinating with the solemnity and rigorous detail of an engineer crafting a device that promised to reverse climate change or a doctor who just wrapped up a groundbreaking surgery in which the heart of a pig was successfully transplanted into the body of a previously critically ill nun, now restored to full health. She couldn't take it seriously.

That was likely why she lost her "real" job in the first place and was now isolating herself inside the "fake" worlds she developed ever so slowly, brick by brick, letter by letter, relegating herself to the possibly meaningless labors of stringing words together into imaginary lives fictional characters could inhabit, realities which felt, increasingly and uncannily so, more actualized than her own. And every once in a while she'd take the scrawls from her physical notebook and use them to draft full pages on digital paper that sat, accumulating, in dead-ended baby blue folders perched atop the default mountains on her laptop's background, containing every bit of what she knew, or thought she knew, to be true. It wasn't very much.

Sitting down, she reflexively opened one of her various social media apps, scrolled for half a minute—artwork of a plexiglass butterfly, woman performing face yoga, selfie of a girl in a purple hoodie, flyer for a reading at eight, selfie of a girl in a black hoodie, ad for virtual reality exercise headset, someone promoting an article they wrote about a fashion show, Édouard Manet's *The Dead Christ with Angels*, foot in a lacy red sock, infographic in various shades of beige—and closed it.

But her phone was like a restless leg. A throb in her hand. Affixed to her face.

She reopened it. Meme about how many times you've had sex this year, person taking a bite of a corn dog, ad for braces that go behind your teeth, guy standing on a mountain, residency program open call announcement, baby in snowsuit, carousel of celebrity courtroom sketches, someone's cat sitting at a piano, before and after pics. She had no idea who any of these accounts belonged to or why she was addicted to looking at their posts. Thankfully, a message from Molly Jane interrupted her scroll, fulfilled Newton's First Law of Motion, stopped her from continuing to tumble insatiably and unceasingly down her feed.

"I know you were skeptical, but have you seen this one?" And a link to a recent interview with Alex Hamberdon on *Last Man Standing*, the once scoffed-at podcast that had now become an outlet for fringe critics and cultural theorists without anywhere else to go, yet whose ideas seemed to be gaining in popularity on, oddly, the outermost ends of both sides of the political spectrum. So the spectrum was a circle, then?

She wasn't sure if Molly Jane's interest in such figures was related to their concepts or the perverse pleasure she got from feeling like she belonged, but only among outcasts and social pariahs. Molly Jane wanted to be someone whose very ideas could be threatening enough to protect her from the dangers of trusting other people. This much was clear from the first moment she heard Molly Jane speak in their poetry workshop and probably had something to do with why Molly Jane dropped out of the MFA just before the end of their first semester.

They both enjoyed the paradox of getting an advanced degree in the most "useless" field possible, so she was surprised when over drinks one day after class Molly Jane said she wouldn't be coming back. "Why not?" she asked, struck by the disappointment she felt over losing her post-workshop gossip buddy. Molly Jane responded with a throw of subtle, unintentional shade, "I don't want to pay to be trained to write a certain way," implying that anyone dumb enough to shell out thousands of dollars for this degree would soon enough be stripped of their own style, the style that got them accepted into the program in the first place. Molly Jane had a similar critique of heteronormative, monogamous relationships, "I feel like both parties end up melding into one person, becoming people who are neither fully themselves. Then you're left with two people who don't know who they are, dating someone other than the person they fell for." She felt defensive but didn't want Molly Jane to know she took it personally. After all, she wasn't exactly monogamous anyway, and she did agree that there was definitely a school of thought (maybe Molly would have called it an "agenda") being propagated, but she kind of enjoyed, found it productive even, having something she could actively push against. She envisioned herself at an awards ceremony in a low-cut gown, hair in an updo, tears in her eyes, giving her acceptance speech: *I'd like to thank the giant chip on my shoulder...*

Poetry certainly was a "pointless" degree insofar as there would never be a financial return on their investments, but she thought that was what they liked about it—finally, something that didn't serve an economic purpose. Molly agreed, but begrudged, understandably, the not insignificant tuition fee. Admittedly, if she'd had to go out of pocket, our protagonist would have never applied in the first place. But her husband paid for her schooling under the false assumption it was going to land her a job teaching back at that same institution which was, conveniently, located within walking distance of their apartment. From a certain vantage point on their roof, one could even see the clocktower with its green-lit belfry and purple turret lights, and the lawn below it, where on nice days her favorite professors sometimes held class, a moveable feast.

Molly Jane took a pull from her vape pen and continued, "Girls like us getting degrees in poetry is a false testament to the advancement of society. They give us room to pontificate on happiness, line breaks, and stardust as if we no longer have to focus on our day-to-day survival. Meanwhile their tuition rates are gonna put me in deep enough debt that I won't be able to afford groceries... Maybe that's their master plan, make us think we're free thinkers but then rob us of any free time to think. I *really* don't want to have to go back to waiting tables."

Molly Jane stayed true to her word and dropped out, but they continued to meet up on a weekly or bi-weekly basis to trade poems, discuss the readings together, and so Molly Jane could scan her notes. It was a fun, victimless crime, a harmless theft harboring this refugee, this nonperson, and the superfluously illicit nature of their dynamic allowed her to savor their secret meetings, which would for no real reason remain that way even after she finished the MFA, letting them echo the kick she got from some of her other, arguably worse habits. But recently Molly Jane had begun to go down a rabbit hole too ideological, the stakes too high, to spark a shared interest.

The last time they'd gotten together, Molly Jane had shown her other videos, loaned her one of Hamberdon's books, and futilely attempted to sway her into synergistic enthusiasm. Maybe she'd come around in a few years, long after Hamberdon had reached mainstream appeal and then disappeared suddenly and inexplicably from public discourse into irrelevancy, after the second wave of Sunnyvale syndrome, once it was still too late. Behind the times, she instead sat with a look of sustained boredom as Molly Jane tried unsuccessfully to ignite a flame of shared passion they could sit and warm their conspiring hands by. But to believe in conspiracy requires faith.

Still, she could, if nothing else, appreciate Molly Jane's tenacity. She clicked the link and, raising her phone to her right ear, Hamberdon spoke:

"...For decades citizens have offered their bodies, data, and identities willingly to the corporations that control our government and virtual networks. We must confront the reality that we have turned to, turned into, AI willingly for the sake of convenience. The time has come, I hope to God it has not already passed, to address what it would take to undo our so-called progress. But I fear that the perceived inconveniences of living without tech will surpass any collective desire to reverse our course of history. It goes without saying that every supposed advancement humanity has made can and has been weaponized against us, whoever 'us' now is.

The industries, corporations, and government structures most often behind the development of these constantly evolving tools were always and will remain primed and positioned, until forcefully removed, to wield these mechanisms over the underclasses. We've seen this happen time and time again. Wearable technology promising an ever-optimized, more healthful existence, for instance, has been utilized by online mega-conglomerates to track the speed and efficiency of underpaid warehouse workers, punishing, threatening, and firing employees who don't comply with productivity levels. Mandatory tracking implants are used to locate and 'relocate' the homeless from upscale neighborhoods to designated encampments—or worse. Sensored medication and medical devices implemented in and outside the body have infantilized those with disability and mental illness, suggesting people with disability or illness are not capable of making their own choices, revoking health care when doctors' orders have not been strictly obeyed. Women in particular have been perfect volunteers to serve at the helm of biotechnical integration—"

The host interjected. "Yeah, um, I wanted to ask you about this, because you've suggested that Sunnyvale syndrome is not naturally occurring, right? What made you..."

"Right. I believe that Sunnyvale is yet another byproduct of humanity's consensual, albeit unwitting, forfeiture of autonomy. Beginning with synthetic beauty implants and enhancements, assistive reproductive technology, and internal security systems, women have made it very easy for nefarious forces to harness information about genetic and behavioral patterns which have led to the further advancement of—"

"I don't know man, my wife just got a boob job and she's fine." The host's laugh made her skin crawl. His voice, that of a generation.

"No, no, no. Hey. I don't think that all synthetic implants or medical and surgical procedures performed on women are resulting in Sunnyvale. They couldn't, the numbers are simply not there, and that kind of one-to-one correlation would be far too obvious. After all, the companies in charge of these technologies don't want the general population to know we've reached singularity, nor do they want us to understand that the singularity has been facilitated by a co-opting of the human mind. If we did, we might be more hesitant and less eager to volunteer our information, our data, our bodies. Nor do I believe all women are susceptible to being turned. According to my thesis there are certain traits that would make it more difficult to manipulate a specimen of control. From my research, I've ascertained that resistance to the bioengineering mechanisms resulting in what we've been calling Sunnyvale syndrome is likely to be observed in those who—"

"Well, wait, one question I had about this theory was about incentive, and who or what would even be determining who gets Sunnyvale. Let's get this straight before the men's rights activists start calling in with their panties in a bunch because their girlfriends won't fuck them because you said—"

There was still twelve minutes left to the video, but she decided that was enough and closed the page.

"Hmmm," she responded, the first of three quick successive bubbles of text. "Isn't it fucked up to blame women when so much of this shit has basically been required of us?" And finally, "I couldn't even watch this whole thing the host is such a pig."

Her bladder was empty by now, but she was enjoying the sound of muffled language and music permeating through the walls and felt hopeful that a moment of privacy might recharge her. She opened the app again, closed it, opened another. *What's happening?* This one prompted. A very good question indeed. She swiped it away and opened her notes.

Writing poems was so much easier than writing stories. This one flowed from her like piss.

It's impossible to say how the idea penetrated my
   brain
But when it sprouts it grows.
Passion. My fetish
For old men. It's because I hope they'll teach me
   something
Or give me money. I like this one
Old man in particular. He never did
Any injustices to me.
He never insulted me
Other than ignore me slightly.
I have no desire to sleep with him again.
But I'd like to look him in my eye.

She stopped tapping at the keyboard, closed her own eyes tightly, and pictured the face of the verging-on-senior editor she fucked a few weeks ago who stopped talking to her abruptly after the fact—probably because he was worried he'd done something wrong or unprofessional or cancellable, which was funny because the only offensive part of his behavior was his pretending it had never happened at all, as if he believed that cold-shouldering her might erase her from existence, undo her, ⌘Z. Did she need to remind him that she wasn't *actually* prepubescent, and was a too easily intrigued adult woman trying to have a good time, and all the better if she could climb a few rungs of this rickety arts professional ladder (which, despite very seriously suspecting it might lead to nowhere, she was disappointed to find herself at the bottom of once again) while she was at it, and avoid the hard prick of rejection, or worse, the desertion of being ignored?—then reopened them.

> Maybe he has defective eyes.
> Blue eyes
> With a film on it. With caution. Look
> How good I work
> On what I want. You should see me. How smart
> I can be. I'll follow him
> For a whole week
> And every night
> Around midnight
> I'll open the phone and open—slowly!

She paused again and looked up at the ceiling. It was unfinished tin, painted many times over in thick black, with a familiar design. Did you know that, similar to counting the rings inside a tree, you can determine for how long and by how many an apartment or commercial space has been occupied by chipping away at the layers of paint or paper that coat the walls? Above her, every square unit of tin contained a circle in a circle in a circle, with little marks that reminded her of holly leaves separating each tier.

> And when my head is open enough, I'll darken,
> I'll disappear into myself. The light will not flash
> And then—oh!
> He'll miss how sexy I am!

Reading through the whole thing quickly, she cocked her head to the side and cracked her neck. A text from Molly Jane appeared above the poem. "I feel like that's kind of missing the point." She brought the cursor back up to the top where she slapdashedly anointed it with a title: "Control machine; or, the victim who was perfectly fine."

"I'm personally more concerned with the fact that they're turning us into robots???"

Clicking her screen shut, a wave of simultaneous accomplishment, disgust, and resentment sprouted inside her abdomen. She stuck her phone in her bra and pulled more toilet paper from the dispenser, the paper reminding her of the coil a magician pulls, supposedly, from the depths of his throat. Wiping from front to back, she could once again hear Mira's words, this time from just a few hours earlier at the bar, breaking through the surface of the poem like a girl catching coins at the bottom of a swimming pool. "What if being a fully formed writer is the assurance of believing one's own bullshit?" Standing up, she used her shoe to kick the toilet paper around the seat into the bowl and rinsed her hands performatively, as if someone were listening with their ear to the door, making sure her ablutions were complete.

When she returned to her seat, her little book was still resting on top of her drink in what, had you asked her, she would have sworn was the same position in which she'd put it down. There was a new group of guys in the corner with full, perspiring glasses in their hands. She shot an arrow across the room, and later, grabbing his shoulder from between her legs, he would emerge from the blanket covered in blood.

Behind the Wheel

Look around. The empty cups. The fog gesturing with its fat fingers, pulling me into her room. The smoke going in and out and in. Strands of light emanating from the street lamps, which I would paint if I could. The greenery uncolored in the night. The cat tiptoeing along the fence, paws stained with wet paint. The plane so small above, making promises. The hair dark on his face and chest and knuckles.

She sits on the couch and he joins her. Their shoes are off. He has black socks on, her feet are bare, toes sparkling. She touches her wrist without thinking. She feels perfectly safe and buzzed from the drinks they had at the bar which hide the circles under her eyes. She rests her glass on a pile of books.

Grabbing his silver zipper, the woman slides down with it. I begin to use my pen strategically, writing with his mouth and bringing one hand to her head as if driving a dirty car. The light in one room turns off and moments later the light in another turns on.

Something About Something

"Everything is so stupid and fucked up," she said between sobs.

Though genuinely crying, she reminded herself of the little girl she'd seen earlier in the day on her walk home from the train, who had stumbled off her scooter and wept for her father's attention, stretching her arms towards him while looking askance in a totally unconvincing performance of self-pity. And now here she was, wet and naked, clinging to her husband's leg. He was sitting on the edge of the tub, she inside, eyes resting on the little chip of imperfect glaze marring the otherwise pristine vessel big enough for two but only ever used by one. He said taking a bath made him feel like a child.

"And there's so much I don't understand," she continued. This was true—the body, politics, love, her own emotions—the latter of which had been placid all day, unfelt, tamped down, and then suddenly explosive, overwhelming in their mysteries.

The crying began after her husband snapped at her, suggesting that she "shut up and listen—he's trying to tell you!" when she paused the documentary they were watching about the Progressive Era and interrupted the voiceover to attempt to ask a question about Teddy Roosevelt, a man whose confounding duality intrigued her. His legacy of fierce masculinity paired with his personal support of women's suffrage...which didn't really become a public position until after his presidency; the way he challenged ideas of limited government and individualism...yet leveraged the power of his personal charisma to win votes; his belief that America should be rebuilt on a foundation of egalitarianism...which could be achieved through imperialist means; his staunch position against slavery...but only because it necessitated having Black people on his sublime American turf; his civic nationalism...versus his white supremacy; his incredible achievements in wildlife protection and conservation...at the expense of the Native Americans who had been stewarding the land for hundreds of years; his promise not to seek a third term...before reneging on that promise and running again four years out of his presidency, as a Progressive... He was in a compelling tug of war with who he was versus who he wanted to be. Which is to say, he was a hypocrite.

The screen was frozen on an image of him speaking into a crowd, finger pointing toward something in the distance, beyond the image's frame. In her mind's eye, this was the position in which every politician from the entirety of history seemed to situate themselves, as if creating the most masterful diversions. She strained her neck, a perfect and impressionable citizen, attempting to behold a glimpse.

She always felt somewhat ashamed pausing the television to ask for clarity on a plot or to briefly discuss her interpretations and assess her husband's level of agreement, which allowed her to better determine her comprehension or adjust her opinions accordingly. Normally, her embarrassment wasn't enough to stop her—curiosity triumphing over irritated sighs or slow, subtly rolling eyes. But she couldn't stand being yelled at. Or, even if she could, she felt she had to pretend that she couldn't.

She'd dropped her fork dramatically onto her plate and stood up, leaving the dinner of chicken parmesan she'd taken over an hour to prepare to go cold. She dropped her phone too, turning what was meant to be a hostile gesture into one of clumsy incapacity, and picked it back up.

In anticipation of her husband coming home, she had organized a triptych of bowls: eggs, flour, and breadcrumbs. Piece by piece, she'd smothered the raw chicken in each ingredient until it was no longer slippery. Then, she had laid the cutlets one by one into the pan half-thinkingly, aware enough of her body only to avoid being burnt, save for the pan's intermittent burp of hot oil. She washed her hands no less than four times throughout the process in a concerted effort to keep the kitchen and their meal uncontaminated, leaving them rough enough that later, grabbing hold of her in bed before closing out the light, her husband would comment, sabotaging his own affectionate gesture, "Geez, you need to put some lotion on those things."

The tv had clashed with the audio from her phone as she cooked, the words melding together into a bland, senseless concoction. It was a type of aversion therapy she conducted upon herself; a controlled overloading of stimuli she hoped would desensitize her to the humdrum pandemonium of contemporary existence, allow her to find silence inside the tumult and thus be able to enter into a trance-like state of quietude at her will. Any day now...

The handle of the cast iron pan scolded but didn't scald her. The pasta boiled as the chicken turned golden as she chopped the lettuce for the salad. A whirling dervish aiming to please. "The way to a man's heart is through his stomach," she once heard on a commercial a million years ago and it stuck. Just as every comment about her own stomach had stuck, i.e.: when walking with her friend Taryn on the beach, two boys looked up at their exposed midriffs, still layered with baby fat, and sang in deep Bill Cosby-esque voices, "J-E-L-L-O," and burst out laughing. She and Taryn completed their walk to their towels from the bathroom boardwalk in silence, wondering who the jingle was being directed at, or if it was intended for them both. Or when her first boyfriend came up with a code word for when, in public, he felt she was eating too much. Or when she was congratulated on her pregnancy at the nail salon, or in the Baskin-Robbins after they asked if she wanted two scoops or three (she decided on zero), or on the street, some random guy yelling behind her, "When are you due? When are you due?!?!" even as her pace indicated she was clearly not pregnant; she was running away. All of the memories compiled into a single document, clipped together so when she pulled on one the rest released like a paper accordion.

She fed the dog. She loved the way he looked at her, like she was God. Spinning around. A top. A dancer. Pulling out drawers and putting back the spatula her grandmother had cooked with, pushing the drawer in with her hip, another hand-me-down. What did her grandmother's mother cook? And her grandmother's mother's mother? Beans, canned salted things. They were poor and happy. "Being poor makes people sick in the head," she, who was once poor, once said.

"So does being rich," he'd replied.

Reaching into the back of the pantry for a jar of tomato sauce, she could see quite clearly the slanting ceiling of the closet of her childhood home, that dark and seemingly bottomless cavity, empty other than pasta and rice and a mess of plastic bags, inviting her in to hide. When she was little she thought she might discover some secret latch back there, a tiny door that would open into a different girl's life, maybe this one. Maybe if she reached far enough past the ten dollar artichokes, truffle oil, and organic sardines their fingers would touch.

Though abandoning her plate was an act of protest, ultimately it would benefit him, since in a few hours, she would return to the table, pick up her dish and bring it to the kitchen where she, in preparation for his tomorrow, would transfer her uneaten dinner to a Tupperware and place it in his lunch bag along with pre-peeled oranges, freshly baked muffins, and pretzels in the shape of braids.

But now she was storming into the bathroom, and she smoked a cigarette while letting the tub fill. The crisp outside air and hot water and smoke blended together into an aroma she'd come to associate with her adulthood. The glow from the apartment window across the shaft filled her with envy and nostalgia, but for what she couldn't pinpoint. Her husband hated when she smoked, probably for the very reasons she enjoyed it. She flicked the butt out the window, stripped, and submerged herself to her chin as she scrolled the news and waited for her husband to come apologize. When he perched himself beside her, she told him to leave her alone and was grateful when he didn't obey.

"I should be allowed to talk in my own home," she said, ending the statement with the upward lilt of a question, averting his gaze by keeping hers on the screen. "I need one place where I can say what I think, or what I think I think, and that place should be my home." She said "my" but he paid the mortgage. He nodded in gentle agreement. Frustrated, feeling both impeded and like an impediment, she shoved a paywalled article in his face about another high-ranking politician and his PerfectCompanion®, adding, "Or maybe you should just get yourself one of these."

He took the phone from her and placed it beside the sink. He looked at her pityingly but knew it was not yet time to speak.

"Do you wish you lived alone? So I wouldn't bother you or interrupt when you're watching?"

Asking this made her feel very small, because while they both knew he would never say so if the answer was yes, she couldn't keep herself from asking. And so it was that their arguments often turned into unproductive rituals of seeking.

He laughed.

Not only were they quite in love, actually, but she cooked his meals and cleaned every dish.

"Of course not. I love you, and I love listening to what you have to say. I just thought you might learn something. I thought you might have your question answered on the show."

The pipes began to hiss and the light in the bathroom gently flickered—an upstairs neighbor must have been beginning their own sequence of nightly rituals.

"Well, was my question answered?"

"What was your question?"

She paused for a moment and then started to cry again, for she'd forgotten what it was she so badly needed to know.

The Daughter Card

Growing up, my father told me stories about her, the bad things she did, and how he protected me from them. Stalker, stranger, actress, guilt-giver. Teacher of all things not to be. A mother without children whose face I might see, flushed and beggarly, in the rare, displaced family photos buried in the bowels of our closets. If I scratched at them, I could practically smell the cigarette smoke coming off her black sweater, her black hair. Lips were sloppy, lacquered with gloss, eyes dark, mascara thick and clotted, Medusa-ends snaked in all directions, creeping free of her. I found myself relieved at the lack of resemblance between us, our only similarities, once I reached a certain age, the huge breasts and the matching wrinkles on our foreheads, between our eyes.

∽

Messages from former high school bullies who, for obvious reasons, want to reconnect, end up in the same strange hidden corner of my inbox as messages from my mom. It's so hidden I can't even find it when I try. When I land there, it's like I'm lost, as if walking through the woods on the side of a highway, or maybe inside of a mirror, looking back on five minutes ago with tears in my eyes.

∽

She'd tightened telephone cords around my father's throat. She'd beaten her fists against my red, half-grown head. She threw tantrums on the front lawn, a woman, feral, as neighbors watched, amazed.

The messages from her date back years, redolent of spam but tear-jerking in their desperation, riddled oddly with typos.

∽

I hate how when you get arrested the officers act all buddy-buddy, like they're envious of your crimes. As if they're on your side, as if you're going to fuck. Or maybe I'm confusing my arrests with my mom's arrests with some shit I saw on tv that happened to me in high school. No, not on tv. Before I was born. Those guys who bullied me, maybe because they wanted to fuck me, grew up to be cops. They got fat and I got a better haircut. Now they send messages inviting me out to the Island to get double-teamed by them and their greaseball friends in the house where they grew up. Thank God I don't drive. Though I did once give head to an off-duty cop I met online from the passenger seat of his Saab. Afterward, we walked around the cemetery. I could tell he wanted me to ask if he'd ever put a bullet in anyone, but I wouldn't give him the satisfaction.

∽

When my mother sends me selfies, I can see our matching eleven lines even in the thumbnail, but when I click the photos to enlarge them, the screen goes black.

∽

The cops would show up to our house on Trinity Lane and she'd play dead. Splayed on the floor, feigning injury, the officers would lift her hand perpendicularly and let it drop. When it fell to the side rather than smacking her in her own face, they would snicker at each other over the wild woman on the living room floor, for they knew she was lying, fully conscious, psychopathic, hysterical, but physically unharmed. I've been told the story so many times I can see it clearly as if I myself were there—playing which role?

∽

When I was arrested upstate for my bad taste in company, they locked me and the friends I was with individually in a row of four holding cells, so we could hear but not see each other, before walking us down to the courthouse in the morning with our hands and feet shackled, extras in a bad Western. To lighten the mood while we waited in our concrete blocks, I charmed my friends with a performance of "Jailhouse Rock." If my dad were there, he'd have leaned over to the cop on duty and filled him in on my adorable adolescent obsession with Elvis. It was puzzling even to me, but I knew I liked his warm smile, the funny way he danced with his legs spread into a wide inverted V that seemed to risk cracking in half with every beat of the drum. I loved the screams in the background of the live recordings. I liked that there were dogs in the songs, and teddy bears. I liked how good he was at standing on his tippy toes. I enjoyed mimicking the snarl of his lip and the exaggerated motions of his famous groin. When I gelled my hair back and impersonated Elvis at a talent show in fourth grade, I wore an oversized T-shirt as a dress with a hem that reached just above my bruised shins. On it, three different colored (green, purple, red) but otherwise identical Elvises overlapped and blended into each other over the words "Shake, Rattle and Roll" as I gyrated like the King for an audience made up of my classmates' gleaming mothers.

Rounds of applause. Standing ovations. "Thank you, thank you very much," I said, in the deepest voice I could muster.

∾

Research Reveals: Children Inherit Intelligence from Their Mother, Not Their Father

9 Magical Pictures of Butterflies Shining Like Rainbows

17 Beautiful Photos of Birds Taking Flight That Will Make You Want to Spread Your Own Wings

∾

At ten, I wrote a novel—it was probably five pages long, memory expands its breadth—about a little girl named Sarah who wanders, transfixed, in an enchanted forest that exists on the other side of her computer. The forest is gorgeous and lush, rife with colors never before seen, filled with limitless delights for all her senses. But once she realizes there's no way home, it doesn't matter how many sweet fruits she can eat from the vine, how many talking animals there are to befriend. She is trapped.

∾

A Hallmark card-style note superimposed over a white bed sheet held up between the pointers and thumbs of a nondescript blonde:

> To my daughter
> *Never forget that*
> *Life* is filled with
> HARD TIMES & GOOD TIMES
> Be brave, be bold and be beautiful
> JUST BE YOUR BEST
> Keep your
> Face to the *sunshine*
> And you cannot see
>   the shadows
> I didn't give you
> *The gift of life*
> *Life* gave me the GIFT of you
> *Life* isn't about waiting for
>   the storm to pass
> It's about learning to dance in the rain
> *Enjoy the ride*
> *And never forget*
> Your way back home

∾

I'm at that age where everyone seems to be getting pregnant. Women who used to post pictures of themselves sucking on the ends of vodka bottles or sitting spread-eagle across the laps of glazed-eyed men now fill my feed with iterations of the same photograph: a husband resting one hand on an expanding belly, the other atop a collie's head. Soon the bellies give way to babies, captured endlessly doing absolutely nothing in new, monumental ways. I like them all—the photos, I mean, and the videos. I don't know the women anymore.

∾

Link to DavesWordsofWisdom.com with the phrase "I Love My Daughter" in thin pink block letters overlaid atop a flaming heart.

∾

Sarah journeys to the edge of the forest only to find an infinite wall of undulating liquid steel, stretching up and down and left and right forever. If only she thought to step through. If only I'd gotten further, I could have written her out.

∾

Photo of a bratty-looking child placing a crown on her head with the words "There Is No Force More Powerful Than a Woman Determined to Rise" in an off-white banner arched above her skull.

∾

Mornings when I'm hungover and scrolling, bearing witness to the nuclear dynamic I myself never had, peering through the window, I crave, along with a burger, a little bit of whatever that is. Maybe if I had a kid of my own I'd stop drinking so much, fucking so much, regretting so much. I'd have something, someone, holding me back from my bad decisions by the apron strings, by the hand. Instead of waking after two hours of sleep with a blaring headache, alone in bed, husband gone for work, I'd be a different person, well-rested and ready to be needed.

∾

Note addressed to the wrong name: "Happy Birthday Sarah. I left you a gifts at your father"s house. No onr. was home. Thr packagr is hnging from thr front door. Rnhiy tbe holidays. livr you much. Mom"

∽

One day I sat down after school at the family desktop to work on my novel and it was gone. Gone. My father must have deleted it in some sort of organizational frenzy, an attempt to tame a reality that was otherwise wholly out of his control. Or maybe he didn't like what he read.

∽

Body of a poem of mine recently published in an online journal. But instead of its given title above it, a kind of new one: "This You."

>   It all begins to feel so
>   regular. 7/11. Fire escape. Time
>   of my life. The murky passenger window
>   of the middle-aged blue
>   Toyota minivan says it all. To snap out
>   I take myself
>   dancing. A song or two, novel, but then I'm all
>   those scenes I've seen,
>   time, again,
>   radio playing a song by Faces or something
>   to that effect. I'm Marlon Brando in the backseat,
>   yelling Stella.
>   Who is Stella? I could have been a
>   we're not taking the picture without Michael
>   in the theater even watching on
>   tv feels amazing but

the scene ends you. I'm talking about me here.
I'm sitting
at work the next day
planning the weekend though I'll
probably get some Funyuns at the gas station,
stay in. A hangover is
or isn't worth the one moment of forgetting
where you grew up, the body hardly.

Underneath: "You sound tired, sleep, not too much, i hope you are doing well. I am always available and I love you very much. i can be reached at 7367320937
I want you to reach me"

∽

My friend, former friend, former best friend, actually, messaged me out of the blue then unfollowed me. Meaning all my messages to her must have started going to that hidden corner, like being in time out, or at the edge of disappearance.

∽

"Girl, Take care of youeself and take precaution against the Syndrome. Very much. Mom"
 "Are you safe healthy well? Stay safe I am here"
 A butterfly emoji next to my name and a video of hundreds of blue tiger butterflies flapping their wings on the branch of a tree, so real they look fake.
 "Message me Please"

∽

The last message Taryn sent before unfollowing was random and unsettling.

Not even a hello, just: "Are you alright?"

"Hey, yeah I'm great, what's up?"

Her daughter was new, I'd been watching her learn to grip objects in her tiny hands and swallow semi-solid food across various social media platforms for the past few months, lending me a fabricated sense of familial care and intimacy. All the pictures and videos were in a recognizable setting, a backyard identical to and just a few miles from where we grew up. I never understood how anyone with a choice would ever willfully decide to stay out in suburbia, where all the houses looked alike and the shopping centers seemed to replicate themselves every couple of miles, a wasteland of chain restaurants and parking lots.

But it was what she wanted her husband to want her to want, who she wanted him to believe her to be.

"I just needed to check in on you. Is everything okay."

Was my sparse social media presence really that concerning? Like, if I don't post, do I even exist? Or was it the fact that I was several years into my marriage but still without children in my profile picture? In hers, she and her husband hold their baby together in their arms. In mine, a younger version of myself stares straight-faced into the camera, body cut below its cleavage.

Affect is hard to read via text. Maybe she didn't have a ton of time, dashed off the question quickly after I flashed into her mind at the sight of a pair of teenage girls sharing an oversized, meat-stuffed sandwich outside the local deli or walking, limbs linked, into the mall. Maybe she was watching tv with her phone in hand while Lila napped in the other room and saw my name in her views, likes.

Anyway, I wanted to ask the same. In all her recent

photos she looked wan and anemic. The vitality that used to beam from her round, cherry cheeks had faded, and her once enviably radiant skin had taken on an ashen tone. "Haha aw, yeah I'm good. Thanks for the concern lol. And how have you been doing??? How's the baby? She's adorable. Can't believe I haven't met her yet. I miss youuuuu."

Seen.

"But seriously, I miss you! Would love to meet Lila."

Seen.

"She looks so much like you. Those lashes."

Seen.

I noticed the unfollow a few days later, so don't know exactly when it was done.

~

Poem with a typo in the title.

For My Daighter:
Mirror, mirror, on the wall...
It does not matter if I'm short or tall...
If I have skinny legs or my hips are wide...
It only matters who I am inside...
When you look at me, don't judge me by my parts...
The most beautiful thing about me is my heart...
Blue eyes, brown eyes, black, or green...
What makes me beautiful...
Cannot be seen...

"I need to know how you are"

~

In the months that follow, I respond to posts of Taryn's

daughter, eventually daughters—"omg she's so cute" "you look so pretty" "heart is melting"—always seen but never acknowledged. It becomes clear that she and her husband share the account, like a heart, or a brain, so I stop writing. There's something eerie about it, not knowing where she ends and he begins.

∽

"I think you appear in this video, Look at it," my mother writes, followed by an emoji with its mouth zippered shut. I click the link but it takes me to a blank white page.

∽

I'm selfish. I want to go to the bar and write. Take a bath in the afternoon. Lay on my back in the middle of the floor, drag myself around the carpet on my belly. I'm a full-grown kid. Having a child might not be such a good idea for me.

∽

"Hi Ms. Blue Eyes your Blue Eyed mother needs to talk to you," the whole sentence hyperlinked to a too-late video of Elvis Presley perspiring, performing "Suspicious Minds," dangerously high on speed in his white bodysuit. The polyester reminds me of a sheriff's uniform.

We're caught in a trap
I can't walk out
Because I love you too much baby...

> Advertisement
>
> # *Your dreams are just a click away.*

04:18PM PT | 11,536 VIEWS

'Controlled by an unknown force':
What it feels like to have Sunnyvale syndrome

BY AMANDA WEISMAN

Barbara Greene, a former elementary school teacher in San Jose, California, was folding laundry when she knew that something was terribly wrong.

"My body shutting down inside me," she said. "Seeing stars. Nausea and dizziness like nothing I'd ever…." Conversations with Greene are punctuated with frequent long pauses and forgetfulness typical of her condition. At the time, she wanted to call to the other room for help, but she couldn't think of the words, and she couldn't move. She said it was as if she were being "controlled by an unknown force." Greene wouldn't learn this until later, but she was among the first victims of a still-inexplicable phenomenon. That phenomenon has come to be known as Sunnyvale syndrome, a mysterious set of symptoms ranging from amnesia to language loss to out-of-body experiences and catatonia, which are often linked to mutations in the brain. By now, Sunnyvale syndrome has afflicted thousands of women globally.

Without any avenues for information Greene felt confused and alone. Now, she says she wants the world to know what happened to her in order to help other women get one step closer to understanding an illness with far-reaching effects. She also wants to raise awareness about the real suffering and injuries behind her condition and says that those who claim this is a case of "girls crying wolf," or who assert that she must be a victim of mass psychosis, are disregarding a real illness with grave repercussions.

In November of last year, Greene gave birth to her first child, and her symptoms started soon after. Initially, she brushed her symptoms off as normal postpartum hormonal changes. She knows now that nothing about it was typical, and her condition continues to worsen nearly one year later. "This is supposed to be the most special time of my life," she said. "But I can't even take care of my child. My child doesn't even know me." Mrs. Greene's husband, Todd Greene, has since hired live-in help to assist with the care of their child and Greene herself.

Though officially diagnosed with an acquired brain injury, the root of the problem remains unidentified. Mrs. Greene expressed frustration at the dearth of information available, as well as her inability to be her own advocate. "The way the doctor explained it to me, he said, it's like I, I, you know...." Without the ability to describe her illness and experience, Mr. Greene facilitated much of our conversation, and Mrs. Greene often echoed his words in the third person: "He said it's as if she has several different parts of her brain blocked out at once." Still, Mrs. Greene feels a sense of urgency in getting her story out to the world despite the challenges she may face in doing so, and explained her desire to speak out about it now because she's "not sure what comes next."

Medical officials have not gathered enough information to state with any confidence what is causing the injuries or what is to blame for their onset, but a report by the National Institute of Health suggested that surgical procedures or the use of anesthesia might trigger chromosomal mutations in those who are predisposed. Others suspect it could be brought on by stress. The U.S. government, which previously referred to Sunnyvale syndrome as an "anomaly," has been subject to criticism from victims who sense a lack of urgency on a national level.

While public anxiety continues to grow, so does the budding trend of online content creators claiming to be victims of the syndrome. Many have drawn scrutiny as attention-seekers whose misrepresentations of the illness can have serious consequences, creating a culture where actual sufferers are met with disbelief and judgment. Still, while it may be easy to dismiss this niche community as chasing fame or followers, the popularity of this subculture hints at an anxiety much more widely felt and experienced. And while the vast array of potential symptoms leaves a lot of room for misdiagnosis, health officials caution that not everyone who displays such symptoms falls under the umbrella of Sunnyvale syndrome.

Social media is also a hotbed for conspiracy theories, ranging from speculations about 5G to bioweaponry to artificial intelligence, all of which seem to be driven by the same sense of social vulnerability and lack of control over world events. However, regardless of how outlandish some of these beliefs may seem, a few experts agree that they don't think this outbreak has manifested naturally. According to Jan Carraway, a spokesperson for the Bureau of Medical Sciences, "There's a lot of literature that indicates that factors such as electromagnetic radiation released by mobile and other communication devices can cause some of these symptoms and signs and brain injuries." Carraway even suggested that there are international and domestic actors who might have the resources "to instrumentalize radiofrequency technology like this in today's world."

Advertisement

New hair.
New you.

When asked about these theories and trends, Mr. Greene said, "People say, you know, it isn't real, it isn't that serious. People tell her, 'Oh, but you look fine.'" To which Mrs. Greene added, "She's not." And a lot of women like her are not.

Another victim, Annabelle Hopkins, served as a speech pathologist until her diagnosis led her to retire early on medical disability. She credits expertise in the field as the reason she has overcome some of the language impairments she has been dealing with since being diagnosed, and has developed strategies for coping, such as keeping a notebook and calendar in each room of the house.

On her day-to-day experience of living with the condition, Mrs. Hopkins says she suffers from blinding headaches, balance issues that lead to nausea, and a fogginess that makes basic tasks difficult, and stated that "Some days I can't get out of bed." It's a struggle for Mrs. Hopkins to remember even the simplest, most basic information, but she acknowledged the support of her husband, who has quit his job to be her full time caretaker.

Mrs. Hopkins, Mrs. Greene, and many others are speaking out against the critics who believe their illnesses result from mass hysteria, citing the confirmable injuries visible on brain scans.

Though Mrs. Hopkins struggled on the phone when asked for a statement, she and her husband subsequently reached out with a joint written statement cautioning against skepticism and urging the public to demand more information from local and state agencies. "We need to humanize this condition so we can stop the spread and start finding a cure. We wouldn't wish this on anyone."

This week, the *Los Angeles Times* stated that there have been suspected cases in Rio de Janeiro, Brazil.

Interlude

I'm eating a twisty donut outside the bodega in the rain when he texts me: "I had a sex dream about you last night."

Cool. Last night I dreamt that there was a guy in my building who was known to be a murderer of women. Either a permanent resident or just passing through. There was an awards ceremony happening on tv, and a few friends and my grandma were over to watch it. My grandma always loved that kind of thing, the red carpet, the stars. But in the dream she was weak and angry and uncomfortable, and most of all, tired of hearing about the man. She sat at my desk and put her head down, like a schoolgirl.

An Orthodox woman with bright orange lipstick jogs past me in her skirt. I watch her dripping reflection disappear beyond the frame of the mirror I was carrying but have rested, for the moment, against a tree. At my feet, stray pages of an abandoned newspaper grow soggy. On it, the dampened faces of protestors appear to be melting below the headline: "World Health Organization chief scientist faces backlash after evidence of Sunnyvale syndrome censorship mounts." Across the street a dog with giant balls assesses the puddle I circumnavigated on the way to fetch breakfast and a pack of cigarettes. Gingko leaves pepper the perimeter. Towards the center they get swallowed up in darkness. His master walks through the puddle, shoes get wet. So do the dog's paws.

I'm afraid I'm incapable of love, I consider texting

back, but instead leave him waiting on those three pulsing dots.

"I was fucking you from behind. It was so good." Blushing emoji.

"I can make your dream a reality," I respond, and it sounds sarcastic. We live together. We sleep parallel in the same bed every night.

"You have such a hot body I want to wrap my arms around you while I cum in your pussy."

It takes me a long time to think of what to say because sexting with your husband is harder than being creative, mysterious, new with a stranger. He's seen it, all of it, the total and utter itness of me, before. This exchange feels disingenuous. An act. Like he could have received an award in my dream while fucking me in his.

"You can cum in me tonight," is the best I can muster with a wet screen and frosting on my fingers.

∾

I carry the mirror above my head, inviting the sky to admire the soft curves and wispy strands of its clouds through the icy veil of glass. The pale sun, what little we have of it in this dark season, disappears as I make my way underground. A cacophony of geese and the ambient hum of a plane recede behind me. Highway sounds drip through the grate. Trucks idling in morning traffic. Orchestra of car horns.

Already, my bladder is full of pressure.

Four stops into my trip the homeless guy who's been shuffling three nickels in his hand and dropping them on the ground, betting in an imaginary game of heads-or-tails Cee-lo, loses against himself, begins aggressively shoving things into his bags, making noise, banging beer bottles on the handrails and opening them with his fuzzy teeth. He stands up, teeters around, and I feel I'm a safe enough distance away to not have to switch cars. I'm glad; lazy, curious, and tired of maneuvering the mirror, about three feet by four feet, framed in heavy teak. I took it down from the wall for money, not considering deeply enough the obtrusive blank space that would be left in its wake or the obnoxious hassle of delivery.

The car says "ooooh" all at once, so I know I've missed something. A woman stands up without her cane and gets up in his face, all her weight on her good leg. I'm guessing he may have hit her or bumped into her in such a way that it was mistaken for a hit, because she won't shut the fuck up, she's moaning and fake crying and there's something wrong with her that has nothing to do with whatever is going on right now.

Two guys flank her, angels on each shoulder, while everyone else relocates to my side of the car. I hold on tightly to the mirror, trying to avoid seven more years of bad luck. The angels demand that he get off at the next stop. She's still moaning like she's lost a child or experiencing a major, catastrophic event and the homeless guy is for some reason saying "thank you thank you thank you thank you thank you." His acceptance speech.

When the train pulls into the station he grabs a hold of his garbage bags and starts to exit. A third guy decides to get involved and kicks him out of the car in a delayed, showy, and obviously unnecessary performance of machismo.

The woman continues her awful howling after he's off the train, making it ever harder to empathize. The angels remind the rest of the ladies on the train that no man should EVER ever EVER hit a woman and they're real men cuz they didn't stand for it and there are good men on the trains, there are good men in the subways, on busses, out in the world on all varieties of public transport. I picture mole people scuttling about in the lower levels, feeling us rumble above them, unaware of our car's grating microdrama.

The guys helped her, sure, and it was good of them, but their announcements strike me as self-indulgent, the way they keep repeating it, their newfound mantra: "No man should ever…ever…ever…hit a woman. Remember that… No man should ever…ever…ever…" As if they need to say it aloud in order to convince themselves of its truth. Turn it into a song with lyrics they can memorize. If I hold the mirror up to their faces while they sing it, will the bloody faces of phantom women appear, their future wives?

Later on, I tell my husband the story while he takes off his socks, pants, work shirt, tossing each layer atop the already overflowing hamper. He doesn't ask about the mirror that's disappeared—or the framed screen print of Adam and Eve that until recently hung above the mantle, or the blown glass vase that used to sit beneath it—and he lacks interest in my anecdote. "I guess you had to be there," I say, and the look in his eye tells me he wonders if we're going to pick up where our morning texts, a lifetime ago, left off. I'm tired and figure we should just wait until the weekend. So I continue talking, pathologizing the men, wondering about the public proclamation of their credo, voicing my suspicions. He sighs.

"You just can't win."

The Mount Sinai Hospital
One Gustave L. Levy Place
New York, NY 10029
212-241-6500

INFORMED CONSENT FOR SURGICAL PROCEDURES

My physician(s) has fully explained to me the condition requiring treatment and the nature, purpose, risk and benefits of the operation(s)/procedure(s), possible alternative methods of treatment, and the possibility of complications. I was given the opportunity to ask questions and any such questions were answered to my satisfaction. No guarantee or assurance has been given by anyone as to the results that may be obtained.

My consent is given with the understanding that any operation or procedure, including anesthesia, involves risks and hazards. These risks can be serious and possibly fatal.

Risks common to all surgical procedures:

- Injury to a blood vessel or excessive bleeding
- Infection, which may require the use of antibiotics. In rare cases, another procedure may be necessary to remove the infection
- Pain after procedure, which may require the use of pain medication

Risks and possible complications of the proposed treatment:

- Recurrence which may require another surgical procedure, or persistent deformity
- Asymmetry
- Problems with muscle weakness, balance, vision, coordination
- Problems with speech, memory and other functions

Surgical operations and special diagnostic or therapeutic procedures all involve risks of complications, serious injury, or death, from both known and unknown causes.

I consent to the performance of operations or other procedures in addition to or different from those now contemplated whether or not arising from presently unforeseen conditions, including the implantation of medical devices, which the physician(s) or his/her associate(s) or assistant(s) may consider necessary or advisable in the course of the operation.

I understand the risks, benefits, and alternatives to the type and method of anesthesia or sedation recommended, and I consent to the administration of such anesthesia as may be considered necessary or advisable by the physician(s) for this surgery/procedure.

I consent to the photographing or videotaping of the surgery or procedure(s) to be performed, including portions of my body for medical, scientific, or educational purposes, provided that my identity is not revealed by the pictures or by descriptive texts accompanying them.

I consent to the presence of observers in the operating room, such as students, medical residents, medical equipment representatives, or other parties approved by my surgeon(s).

I consent to the disposal of any human tissue or body part which may be removed during the surgery/procedure(s).

I have been advised that there is a possibility of unforeseen damage during surgery and administration of anesthesia, and I waive any claim for damage as a result thereof.

I understand that, unless instructed otherwise, I am required to have a responsible adult accompany me after my surgery/procedure(s) and that I will be released to that person's custody, and must rely upon him/her for my return home and supervision, as instructed.

I understand that if I am pregnant, or if there is the possibility that I may be pregnant, I must inform the surgery center immediately since the scheduled surgery/procedure(s) could cause harm to my (unborn) child or myself.

My signature below constitutes my acknowledgment that:
1. I have read, understand and agree to the foregoing;
2. The proposed surgery/procedure(s) have been satisfactorily explained to me and that I have all of the information that I desire;
3. I hereby give my authorization and consent.

Patient Signature: _____

Surgeon's Attestation: Prior to the procedure, I discussed the condition requiring treatment and the purpose, risks, and benefits of the operation(s), surgery/procedure(s), possible alternative methods of treatment, including non-treatment, and the possibility of complications with my patient or the patient's authorized representatives. I provided my patient or his/her representative with the opportunity to ask questions and answered all questions to their apparent satisfaction. I have reviewed the surgical consent form and verified that the planned surgery/procedure is accurate.

Surgeon's initials: _____

The Lunch Crowd at Rick's

She puts three cherries in my drink I didn't ask for and gives a lesson on etiquette: "Approach the stage to tip. Or beckon them with a finger and put the money in their shoes." She pats my hand. "They'll be milling around."

It's two p.m. on a Tuesday in mid-December and I'm one of five customers. I'm the only woman in a sweater and the only person taking notes.

The stage is decorated with a miniature sleigh filled with empty boxes, absent of gifts. A pair of spiky plastic pine trees, also miniature, sit at the edge of the stage and a big gold bow hangs precariously from a mirror to the side. A giant wreath dangles above the dance floor and tinsel and multi-colored lights line the staircase at stage left, circling up to the third floor, where the private rooms are. There's no pole, not on stage, just an acrylic dance floor and mirrors all around, smudged top to bottom with oils from her body.

Hope, Hope, welcome Hope to the stage next.

The best performers make me feel like I'm the only one in the room, even if intellectually I know that from where she stands, I'm nothing more than a pair of floating eyes in a dark pit of dollars.

Still, here, a smile makes me feel special and feeling special makes me feel shy. A smile is pregnant with implication and the implication is a fiction.

～

I get a lap dance from a stripper named Phoenix. She's pretty and petite and smells of a department store. Backlit and above me, I get a twinge of guilt while I awkwardly decide where to place my hands. Her face reminds me of Ginny's, and I'm reminded of the ease with which I let my friendships fade and fall into the background, as if they were merely markers of personal development, shadows of past lives.

I grab a gentle hold of her waist, where it dips in like the sides of a figure eight. "Phoenix," I say, wondering why she chose a name so heavy. Almost taunting in the context of a strip club, where the last thing you want to associate with a dancer is the trauma they overcame from their past, the fires from out of which they rose, renewed, only to end up back here, in this ashy dungeon, leaning into your undeserving arms. "You can stop." But she doesn't.

The dance is a gift from the owner of the club who has taken an interest in my notebook. He told me I could have as many drinks as I want, on him. An offer I overzealously accept. Someone else's body and I take. She disperses her pheromones onto me. Fairy dust. A stark counterpoint: he sits in the corner sweating into his nachos, bossing people around, occasionally glancing up.

The tv is on. Three, actually. Never not something flashing.

Stock market (up). Basketball (losing). And the news, a hailstorm, the latest syndrome numbers, nuclear deals, delays, seizures. Static verbs, promises undelivered. Turn it off.

∽

She wants to know what I'm writing. "Nothing yet. I was uninspired," I say, "and found myself here."

"Aww," she says. "I love that."

Why does it get so hard? Hard to speak when I feel shy.

"What do you write?"

"Poetry mostly, but lately I've been trying to write stories. For instance, I have one about a woman with alphabetical limbs and another about a girl who looks too deeply in the mirror. What do you think I should write about?"

"Here? Well, it really is different every day, and there's no one type of guy..."

"Maybe not." But we could probably count the types on our combined fingers.

I wait for her to take my hand in hers, intertwine them into a fist. Obviously, that doesn't happen.

"They do all seem to lurk in the shadows, though."

Obviously, she doesn't answer.

I wouldn't mind being less seen, myself.

"I wish us girls had a place to go like this," she says.

Never mind that we're both already here.

"Where the men would have to serve us, where the men would have to—"

∽

Phoenix is on stage, and Hope has taken her place next to me.

"I'm so gullible," I confess. "When you smiled at me from up there, it made me feel warm inside." I thought maybe I was different because I'm a woman, but she's clearly just doing her job, and I may as well be one of them.

In fact, I might be worse. Because I understand the rules of the game, and I want her to convince me they're otherwise. I feel as if I'm reminding a withholding boyfriend to tell me he loves me, only me, only ever me.

"I was never much of a hustler. When I smile, it's because I want to smile. I'm smiling because it makes me feel good to make someone else feel good. When you smiled back, it made me feel good too."

She does it again, looking up coyly and convincingly. Maybe we'll exchange numbers and get together after her shift at a bar with better airflow to discuss, conspiratorially, how much she made from the afternoon's pudgy pool of suckers.

I never thought of smiling as a type of hustle before but she's right. She's absolutely right. You attract more flies with honey…Honey…Honey approaching the stage…

∽

"So you're a writer?"

"Among other things. Is this your only job?"

"No, I'm a realtor and a model."

The connection between her various gigs isn't lost on me. Against the sound of clacking hooves, high heels, I imagine her holding the door open for home-seeking couples, welcoming them into the bare interiors of unoccupied condos in high-rise buildings that prick the clouds, windows that reach the ceiling casting a film of sunlight over the marble tiled floor. She taps across it like the dancer she is, encouraging them to picture the view as their own, to imagine the place stuffed, like bills in a G-string, wall to wall with their shit.

"I'm not surprised," I say, "your smile must look great on camera." Pressing a button, I've prompted her to bare her teeth yet again. I resist the urge to apologize.

"Are you published?"

"Yeah, here and there."

"In magazines or online?"

"A bit of both." I feel pretentious and also like a liar.

"I hope you make a lot of money."

"Do you?"

"Sometimes you get lucky."

"Have you ever gotten involved with anyone from the club? Romantically?"

"I'm engaged to a former customer, actually. But I don't tell the shadows that. I don't want them to think...well...I do and I don't."

Compulsively, my eyes scan the row of screens.

Stocks are mostly rising as investors elude syndrome risks. WNBA cancellations and forfeitures announced. Good news, bad news, and what it all means—for you.

Me?

Her name emanates from the speaker once again, and she dutifully gets up from my side, gives me a kiss on the cheek (I can't tell in this fantasy if I'm the daughter, the father, or the best friend), and begins making her way back to the front of the room. She walks up the stairs to the stage like a priestess to her pulpit, ready to perform her sacred rituals. Jason Diamond slides onto the empty barstool, vinyl still warm from her ass.

∽

"I'm Jason Diamond and I recently retired from writing. I used to write lyrics and speeches. I wrote things I'm not allowed to talk about. I wrote things that made me a lot of money, and I'm not allowed to talk about any of it. What are you writing? Tell me."

Jason Diamond looks into, or possibly through, my face. A shiny, inebriated, bizarro Clark Kent, Jason's powers include a highly durable ego invulnerable to my, under normal circumstances, conversation-ending responses and body language suggestive of the room I need a little more of. Unfortunately, Jason Diamond wants to know my story. Needs to know my story. He pretty much tells me my story.

"You're here alone on a weekday afternoon watching women dance while drinking Manhattans and writing in your book. What are you writing?" he asks again. "I need to know. Please tell me. I wanna read it so bad. Who are you? I need to know. Please tell me. Can I back you up? Your drink, when you're ready."

I tell him that's not necessary since I'm not paying for my drinks anyway, but it doesn't matter. He stands up and hovers above me like a buzzing drone, over-gesticulating to the bartender. I can smell his cologne. Axe. High school. I hate that I like it, but it's not my choice, the flick to that switch buried deeply in my hippocampus yet so easy for him to turn on (is this why the girls wear so much perfume?). I'm in the woods on the side of the highway in a clearing of trees drinking beer and feeling rebellious. I'm in the sump by the mall letting him put his hands, with their yellowed fingertips, up my pink and black polka dot mini skirt, hem of faux lace grazing his forearms. I'm in my friend's basement asking her older brother to get us a dime bag, hoping he'll smoke it with us. I'm at the playground at midnight, the beach at four a.m., empty cans speckled about like confetti. We're on his bed making out, fully lost in each other's mouths, resurfacing whenever we think we hear a door open or close, whenever we think those might be his mom's footsteps on the stairs. I'm sitting up, nauseous.

If I stay here much longer I might turn into a pumpkin. It's no longer the afternoon and the crowd is changing and I'm getting cranky. I'm getting paranoid. With an absent-minded swing of an arm, Jason breaks a glass. "I'm so sorry. I got nervous. It was her."

Me?

"She made me nervous."

Jason smiles at me as if I'm his accomplice. He's using me to flirt with the bartender.

"I'll pay for it…I'll pay for it…"

༄

Jason, how did you become a regular?

"I'm in love with the bartender, her tight body. Look at her body," he says, and I do.

How did you become a shadow, Jason? How do I?

"Just do what I did. I wasn't worried about it and you shouldn't either."

Worry about what? You're slurring your words, Jason.

"Are you in love with anyone?"

"Yes," I say, "I'm married." But I don't explain the rest.

༄

Jason made millions writing lyrics. Jason retired. Jason follows the girls with his eyes. Jason acts like he owns the place. Jason says we're very similar, we're starving artists. Jason looks at his watch and I'm confused by what he means. The steel links are cold around his wrist, the hands touch every second of the day.

Jason says we're all trying to write the Great American Novel. We all have something new to say. I correct him: we all think we have something new to say. "What are you writing?" he begs. He doesn't want to read; he wants to win. He asks me questions so he can answer them himself. I'm his little echo chamber and he wants to see me naked because I'm the only woman here wearing clothes.

"Show me what you're writing," he says. "Now. I'm serious."

I hand him my book and he reads a few lines and pushes it away. He looks upset. His feelings are hurt. I'm sorry, Jason.

"And you're fucking married? No. Just no."

I flip to a page from earlier in the day, tear it out, fold it up, and slide it, suggestively, into his pant pocket. "For you, for later," I tell him. For reasons unknown, I'm either scared of him being mad at me or eager to maintain his interest. It makes no difference. He'll forget what I've given him and feed it to the washing machine.

"Make Jason a monster in your story," the server jokes.

∾

I take my socks off, make myself ten pounds lighter, put a few dabs of my grandmother's Jean Naté on each wrist: sun-warmed citrus, a walk through the back woods holding her soft-as-petals hand, notes of lavender hiding behind a neck dusted with baby powder, open-palmed geraniums on the sill while baking in the kitchen, small red roses and white spring flowers making kissy faces outside the window. Get up on stage. "Bad Guy" plays and I sway my hips, bound in the gesture of a corset, a cupless bra.

I see now what the girls have been looking at all day. Monsters in leather shoes and collared shirts the color of swamps protecting chalky, sallow skin. Politicians with glossy teeth and big heads. Stockbrokers traveling the multiverse of the city seeking subjects of amusement which they can add to their collection of captured worlds. Evil scientists in camouflage, infatuated with ruling the planet. Lawyers with the ability to absorb their victims' strength and knowledge through touch. Doctors aiming to annihilate every minor imperfection. Fraudulent and failed heroes of post-syndrome Earth lamenting their lost fate as protectors of the universe. Parasites eager to propagate, and who do so by injecting themselves into the bodies of warm, fleshy things. Power-hungry imps with cannons capable of firing high-energy projectiles. Ravenous fiends who feed off those who wander into bars alone.

Usually you can avoid them by going out only in daylight or remaining completely still. Alternatively, you can use a bow and arrow to shoot into their empty cores. If they have a chance to fight, they will. Just remember to stay on your knees, near their weak points. Destroy them by burning them to pieces, or protect yourself with something piercing, like the tip of a pen. Larger than the average woman, their flashing eyes bring about storms of ice, cracking mountains in half. The broken mountains reveal dark galaxies inside, made of money. When the song ends, pull a wad out from the middle and leave it on the bar.

No one told me how to deal with my anger
but did I cry about it?

I tried to move slowly so that his sleep
would not be disturbed.

First, I learned to like the faint, boring, crackling
sound in my ears, like a needle in a cotton ball.
But it gets louder and louder like a drum.

My old man sat up in the bed
and shouted: "Who is it?"

It seemed an hour, to get from the kitchen
to the bedroom door. Ha! I'm crazy
and my phantom head follows me into every room.

The seconds pass. The yellow from the street lamps
shakes in fractured loops, rings fall
from my thin fingers, giving me away.

I was silent and said nothing,
for I did not want to tell a lie.

He was still sitting on the bed, listening, scared,
    like me.

I ordered a steak

Bloody and buttery

How is it, love?

I wish it weren't

So big and fat across my plate

The Enchanted Forest

CHAPTER 1   Have you ever been stranded all alone with creepy eyes watching you, asking yourself what do I do now? Ever felt the waves of trees over you and felt the wind in your hair? Have your fingers ever sank into the moss? Has your hand crossed the big oak tree?

When she looks around she sees all the colors of the rainbow, and more. She follows the wild animals, can see all their movements as if they didn't care she was there. She looks inside the dark eyes of the caves, sleeps on soft yellow pine needles. She's breathed sighs of relief and gasps of fear and seen the silence of the forest as a gift, and then a curse.

CHAPTER 2   Unusual shadows cover the forest floor. She treats the forest like the inside of a pocket, every river or rock and every oak or pine or beech and every speck of dirt is inside the bottom of the pocket and she can't reach out. At first she liked to stay there, sleep with her favorite blanket made of fuzzy leaves and drink ice water from fresh springs. But now she sighs and puts herself in the shade of the tree and spends another day thinking of life back home. If only there was somewhere between here and there. Her name is Sarah and let me start from the beginning.

CHAPTER 3 Sarah lived with her mother and father. One day Sarah's mom helped her pack a lunch box and brought a blanket into the backyard for her. She laid on the blanket looking at the shapes in the clouds. Hands waving hello, a turtle in its shell, and a girl with a cape were some of the things she saw.

After finishing her carrots she went inside to do her homework. Her eyes were tired from looking at the blue sky. She felt like if she went in a room with no windows, her eyes would glow in the dark. She fell asleep with the computer on. It was making a buzzing sound like a bee. In her dream she was floating, out through the window, over the top of the fence and up above her town, she even yelled hello down to her neighbors, but she was so high up they couldn't hear her. When she woke up she wasn't at her computer anymore. She was in the middle of a big field that looked like her screen saver. The sky was even bluer than earlier and farther away there were trees. She walked towards them and into a forest. Sarah was amazed because there were beautiful butterflies all of these colors she never saw before, and there were cute monkeys, fast-flying birds with purple feathers and amazing creatures of all kinds! There were bushes that had funny looking fruits and berries dangling from them and the grass was soft as animal fur and it felt like she was in a movie and everything looked brighter but Sarah didn't pluck any off the bushes because she wasn't sure if something might be poisonous.

Then a little creature landed on Sarah's shoulder. It

was talking loudly but in a language she couldn't understand. It plucked one of the beans off a bush and handed it to her. It was shining. She didn't want to be rude so she swallowed the bean which had a candy taste and she could have eaten a hundred. All of a sudden after eating she could understand every word the creature said! It laughed, "Welcome to the Enchanted Forest! This is the adventure of a lifetime!"

Sarah said hi and asked, "How did I get here?"

It replied, "You're going to have to figure that out on your own! That's part of the adventure!"

So she said, "What should I do first? How long have I been here?" It didn't answer. Instead it handed her some pink and purple ribbons. Sarah didn't know what they were for so she put them in her pocket but then the creature had tears in its eyes.

"You're supposed to wear them like a necklace," it told her. The creature showed Sarah how to tie them on. It reminded her of the necklace she got for her birthday. She didn't like wearing jewelry but she felt bad so she wore it anyway, even though it made her feel like someone else. "Don't be in such a rush to go home, Sarah!" the creature said.

"I'm not," Sarah said, but then it made her think of her house and parents and school and teachers and dog and it made her worried they were worried. She wanted to explore the forest though and told the creature, "I've only been here a little while it's okay."

"There are no wonders like the wonders in the Enchanted Forest! Here, drink this," it said, pulling down a leaf with clear droplets inside. She thought it was water but it tasted sweeter than anything she ever had and one sip led to another and it was everywhere.

CHAPTER 4 She kept on walking and walking and her legs weren't tired. Every step she took she saw new animals, the cutest things she had ever seen! And whenever the sun started to set she could look behind a leaf and find a flashlight. Whenever she wanted to read she could reach inside a tree trunk and pull out a book and a candle. When she was thirsty the leaves were always full and when she was hungry the fruits fell off the branches. When Sarah wanted a friend all she needed to do was clap her hands and little creatures would run up to her to play. "It's so nice to see you!" they would say, hugging her as if they had known her a very long time.

CHAPTER 5 It had been a few days and Sarah was having so much fun! But then one of the creatures asked her if there were creatures like him where she came from and she told him about birds and squirrels and the rabbit in her classroom. "Do you miss them?" the creature asked and she thought of her dog licking her face and sitting on her lap and she started to feel bad because she had been so distracted by the colors and the creatures and the beans that tasted like candy that she hadn't really been thinking about home that much, it really was the adventure of a lifetime!

"Oh yes, terribly," Sarah said. "Maybe I should call my mom?" she asked the creature but he just smiled at her and said he didn't know what that meant. She knew he was lying because she had just eaten a big glowing bean. Then she ate another glowing bean just to make sure but the creatures pretended not to know the words. One of the creatures handed her one more bean. She ate it, thinking it would make them understand her. Instead it made her very tired. Her eyes got heavier and heavier until she started to fall asleep. In her dream, there was one creature who looked the same as her. It told her to find the purple and green sign near the tall steps. The creature pulled her necklaces but couldn't get them off. It held her hand and then let go.

When she woke up her shoes were off and the leaves from the trees were fallen over her like a blanket. It seemed it had rained but none of her clothes were wet and the sun was out like every other day, everything felt very calm. Sarah stood up and shook the ropes of vines, and they shuffled. Someone was laughing and dropped some delicious beans. She stopped in the middle of chewing and spit them out, even though she was hungry. She had a feeling if she ate the beans she wouldn't be able to find the purple and green sign.

CHAPTER 6 It seemed she had walked for miles and saw everything there was to see, until things started to look like they were repeating and she thought maybe she was back at the beginning again. The wind started blowing harder, and it got harder to move and pushed the water back inside her eyes. "Sarah," Sarah said to herself and her voice cracked. "Sarah. Are you dead?" It wasn't funny, but she laughed, a bad laugh, her heart was beating really loud. They all laughed, all the birds and creatures and monkeys and animals that were supposed to be her friends.

CHAPTER 7 All of a sudden she turned a corner and there was a castle with windows made of gold. There was a party, and smiling faces, and the music was low, and there were laughing children. It was really surprising to see this, because she thought she was the only human here. Every time someone opened the front door, the smell from outside came in. It was nice but something was weird. It didn't seem enchanted like the rest of the Enchanted Forest.

The clock struck like a hammer and everything in the world of the Enchanted Forest glowed as if it were lit up from outside, a giant lightbulb. It was two o'clock and she was drinking freshly squeezed orange juice and there were also waffles and Sarah was starting to feel happy again because she was getting sick of the fruit and glowing beans, even though they tasted like candy.

"Look out the window," a girl said to her and pointed to a pair of striped unicorns. Then she pointed to an ocean and said they can go swimming with dolphins, whales, friendly seals and other fish. She pointed to a coconut tree and said there was some coconut juice she could drink straight from the trunk.

"I never had coconut juice before," Sarah told the girl.

"You can have whatever you want here, you just have to think it."

"Can I call my mom? I don't want her to worry," Sarah asked but then the girl looked upset.

CHAPTER 8   An hour or two hours must have passed and Sarah said goodbye to her new friends and promised to come back soon. She wanted to be able to come back but she also wanted to find the purple and green sign. When she walked outside the sky started spinning and changing all its colors and she wasn't sure what direction she should walk anymore.

CHAPTER 9   She crawled into a secret hiding place in a tree. In the tree she couldn't move much, but she had some pens and pencils she took from her school bag. She wrote in her journal and looked at the walls reflecting all of the twisting hard roots. She began to sketch images of wild leaves and flowers, all pictures of things that she had never been able to see or draw before she got there. She touched the walls of the hiding place and the walls were hot, maybe there was a fire underneath keeping all of the roots warm. A little while after that she fell asleep and she thought of being home and pretended someone was tucking her in and she fell asleep.

CHAPTER 10   Sarah woke up hungry and imagined that the beans were chocolate cake for breakfast. She fed a rabbit and a chipmunk and headed off on her journey. There were small drops falling for the first time, and there was a terrible cloud in the sky towards the north. Sarah felt dizzy and hot, but she could sense where she needed to go. And she turned and ran and kept running as fast as she could, she felt like someone was following her.

CHAPTER 11   Sarah fell and scraped her knee. It was bleeding a little and dirty. She looked around and saw faces looking at her. She stood up and leaned against a tree even though her legs were shaking. She turned around and saw a big gray wolf approaching. She almost screamed but he said, "You don't need to be scared."

CHAPTER 12   The black and brown eagle hides in its feathers. The fox is bright and calm. The lynx has light eyes and knotty woven fur. The owl has red and yellow eyes. They say they saw Sarah running and wanted to help her. "But I'm fine," Sarah told them. Sarah grabbed a leaf and poured some water on her cut, and the blood and scrape disappeared. "See?" she said but then the wolf stood on a stone and spoke.

"Brothers and sisters. Five hunters of the Enchanted Forest have gathered here today to help Sarah."

"I'm okay," Sarah said. Her new friends looked at her.

Then Eagle said, "I'm an eagle with a very sharp eye, I'll be watching over you." It flew over her and dropped a feather, and when the feather fell on the rock it gave a little spark.

"I'm a fox, my cunning is my ability." He jumped over the rocks and a spark escaped from below his toes as he landed.

"I'm a lynx, I can jump too."

"I'm an owl, I can see at night." There was the sound of a trumpet from his chest. Then the wolf roared.

"Do you know what it is you are looking for?" Wolf asked, and before she answered out loud he said, "We can help you, but you may not like what you find." How did he know? "I can read the thoughts of others," he replied. She bowed her head. She didn't seem to be in control of herself. She was really confused. "Sarah, look at your hands," Wolf said. She could see shapes in the trees and could hear a buzz of cicadas and could hear fur rustling and smell the earth. She looked down and gasped. She stood on all fours and saw furry feet under her.

CHAPTER 13 She was a beautiful snow leopard with a white fluffy face. She let out a big roar and then sat down without saying another word. Wolf spoke. "Did you know we have powers? Owl can see through objects. Eagle can fly at speeds of up to two hundred miles per hour. Cougar has super strength. Lynx's roar can deafen your ears, and I can jump so far and read minds." Sarah didn't speak but he answered what she was thinking.

"You can be invisible," Wolf said.

Without saying another word, Sarah turned around to run. She jumped, jumped, jumped, ran and wandered. She never felt such power and grace. The five hunters followed and together they went to the top of a mountain, they climbed a cliff and talked to the moon, they saw water below them so far away at the ocean. In the distance she could see the purple and green sign. "Follow me!" Wolf said because he knew how to get there and she wanted to go.

CHAPTER 14 When they got there they passed the sign and there was a huge wall and it was like looking in a gray and blue mirror. The wall went up and down and side to side as far as the eye could see. The sun was going down and the sky was a beautiful pink. All of a sudden she fell on all fours. She had no long nails, no fur, no tail. She became human again. Her heart was pounding and her muscles were shaking from running so much. "Look," said Wolf and he pointed to the wall she could see through now, and it showed her house on the other side. Sarah stared at it so confused. She saw herself standing on the other side, and her mother and father, they were all talking and acting like she wasn't even gone. Her heart was pounding. "You know what this means, don't you?" Wolf asked.

The sun was going down and she could feel her tail growing again. She was shocked and couldn't speak. "Cat got your tongue?" Wolf laughed.

On the other side of the screen her mom was whispering in the other Sarah's ear. "Do not panic my dear, no one will hurt you." It was

Patient 8245VIH-XMW7627   Close this window

AFTER VISIT SUMMARY

Administered by Laurence Mitchel Sartor, MD

Medications Given

- dexmedeTOMIDine in 0.9 % sodium chloride (PRECEDEX) Stopped 1:34 PM
- electrolyte-A (PLASMALYTE) Stopped 1:38 PM
- fentanyl Last given 12:57 PM
- midazolam (PF) (VERSED) Last given 1:06 PM
- ondansetron (ZOFRAN) Last given 1:25 PM

What's Next

You currently have no upcoming appointments scheduled.

Get Smart

You have just filled a prescription for a controlled substance.

Read This Important Information

- Take it exactly as your medical expert tells you
- Do not skip doses
- Do not share it with others
- Finish the prescription even if you feel better
- Do not save it for later

Why is this checklist so important?

Using prescriptions the wrong way can make your condition harder to treat and can be dangerous unless used as directed. You can prevent this problem by getting smart about your prescription.

TAKE YOUR PRESCRIPTION AS DIRECTED.

For more information call 800-CDC-INFO or visit
www.cdc.gov/getsmart/community

MyHealth® licensed from Epic Systems Corporation

Contact Call

She arranged the bundles of cockscomb and amaranth she'd gotten earlier at the twenty-four-hour market among three vases and placed them in the kitchen, living room, and bedroom. She enjoyed picking types and colors that seemed as if they could be from another planet, a different world entirely, somewhere far from her corner desk with thick pieces of folded paper steadying the legs and bathroom that couldn't ever get truly clean and kitchen where, like a frail Sisyphus, she cooked the food and washed the dishes in an endless loop.

All day seemed to be spent this way, wandering from room to room, a dog chasing its own tail, growing frightened every so often at sudden shapes made on the wall by shadows, or getting startled at an unexpected bang from a car backfiring, an upstairs neighbor dropping their phone, interrupting her quiet solitude as she killed time waiting for her husband to get home so she could paw at his leg.

For now, she used a free hand to pull out her little vial from the drug drawer.

It was a sunny but windy Thursday and she had a million justifications for why it was and was not a good idea to get high alone on this particular fall evening. She took the vial over to the couch and placed it on the coffee table where she rested her feet, alternating her gaze between the minuscule glass jar (how could something so small contain so much power?) and her red toenails while she ate a bowl of nearly flavorless Heritage Flakes and half contemplated, half let her mind rest. Doing drugs always seemed in the service of one of two things: activating her brain to let her thinking run amok or to clear her head and go totally blank. Right now, it was squarely in the middle, and she was bored and longing, eager to push herself in any direction, preferably up.

It wasn't even five p.m., but it was getting darker earlier, so she needed to make a decision quickly because she wanted to get high while it was still light out if she was going to get high at all. She put the bowl on the side table and turned on the tv, which was so loud and abrasive she immediately turned it back off, determining her course of action. She poured the powder onto the cover of *Eros in Antiquity*, a book plucked from the shelves in her grandmother's basement almost two decades ago—where had the time gone?—which now doubled as a giant coaster, and broke out two long lines.

~

Through experience, she'd come to learn that the first line never really did much for her, so she waited only until she felt the drip in the back of her throat from the first before doing the second.

Ah, there it was.

The room got longer, or maybe her limbs got longer, and she crawled onto the carpet, slowly, and grabbed the tennis ball that had rolled under the tv console. Her skin was hot, hot on the inside, and she felt the tension releasing, the poison in her upper back, hips, and glutes dissipating as she rested it under various parts of her body. She did this for a few minutes, moaning on the living room floor, each micro-movement opening up and revealing hidden pockets of heat and anxiety buried in the deep spaces between her muscles and her bones.

"Trauma is stored in the body," she could hear Molly Jane say. Molly Jane, who wore animal print cowboy hats and dog collars, did her makeup with huge pink dots on her cheeks and in the shape of a heart on her lips to look purposefully like a human doll, who believed in aliens, crystal healing, ayurvedic eating (when she could be convinced to eat at all), and who, despite being probably one hundred pounds, could and would regularly consume magic mushrooms in handfuls as if they were raw unsalted almonds. She wanted to laugh at her friend's theories, but whenever she followed the little gluten-free breadcrumbs—5G, reptilian elite, fluoride in the water, big pharma, big tech—none of it seemed all that funny or far-fetched. Maybe it was just Molly Jane's delivery, the way she shared her views both as information and as unanswerable questions, that didn't leave her entirely convinced. She figured that if Molly Jane had stayed in the program, she would have learned to speak with more authority. How concerning to think that presentation was really at the heart of so much of what was commonly accepted as fact. "And what the fuck is that about?" Her friend's voice, along with so many others, lived rent-free inside her head. "Who designed suits, envelopes, municipal buildings?"

Maybe that was what she liked about Molly Jane, who didn't use conversations merely as a method to get people to agree with pre-formulated ideas already set in stone. Discovery through discourse was possible, and unlike so many of the intellectuals and pseudo-intellectuals in her vague orbit, their frequent debates and dialogues were flexible, agile, and surprising, because the one thing they both knew for sure was that they weren't sure of anything. That they could be convinced of each other's positions was a testament to both their gullibility and their open-mindedness.

Then, out of nowhere: "Siri, play 'Peace Frog.'" Her own voice, its reverberations, surprised her. Speaking had nearly no sensation, which misaligned with all its powers.

She was discovering the song for the first time, again. Drugs were worth doing for this side effect alone, if for no other reason at all. How often, after seeing a brilliant movie, reading a perspective-shifting book, or hearing a very funny joke, did she feel a sense of disappointment, grief almost, knowing she would never be able to experience it that way again. She wished she had a memory eraser, like that drink they served her in Memphis, or the pen-sized device in *Men in Black*, which she could shine in her own eyes in order to wipe clean her knowledge of her favorite things, just so she could imbibe them again, anew. Of course, she'd keep a list with a leading title in her nightstand drawer that she would find before bed, digging around for her moisturizer, taking her down what would seem, wrongly, to be a path never before traversed.

"Siri, turn it up." "Siri, louder." She stood and danced like a madwoman around the living room. It felt really good to have a body right now, and when the song ended in its abrupt way, she demanded it once more—jumping, gyrating, and shaking her hair around the apartment, not once paying mind to her downstairs neighbors who were probably returning from work or preparing dinner or waking up for their night shift or fighting with their children or trying to hear their show or attempting to wind down from a long, tiresome day with a vice of their choosing, which she, unaware and in absentia, was rudely interrupting.

And yet ironically, this had to be the meaning of life—effervescent moments of blissful unthinking, freed from anxiety and dread, conscious of no one but oneself. Last night she cried for no reason in particular while lying atop her husband on the couch. The day had been wholly unspectacular and inoffensive, but it felt like she was tugging on a disappearing rope. Her head was impossibly heavy, and even when her smile was hiding, the marionette lines on her face indicated that so much time had passed, which was strange because the words and days were not very long. She guessed with resignation that she was sort of depressed, so incredibly tired, yet something in her kept resisting sleep, only aggravating the problem. She couldn't think straight. In the back of her mind was always her grandma, sitting in a dark room waiting for the phone to ring. The staff knocking on her door about dinner time. The tv's glare reflecting on the windows at dusk, another iteration of itself. In such cases, one couldn't know which was more real or unreal than the other. Her melancholy filled her with guilt; she knew she was quote unquote very lucky.

Whatever. She didn't need to have a reason. She just felt like bawling.

Her husband stroked her hair and told her it was okay to cry, but she should try not to get so "wound up." She knew what he meant, but the phrase bothered her. Like she was a toy. One of those ballerinas stuck in silence in that tiny box, the music only starting when someone's big fumbling hands would break open her room, their eyes landing upon her, her cue to perform. She collected herself, got up to blow her nose, and he joined her in the bathroom to brush his teeth.

"Don't you ever want to cry like that?" she asked.

"Why should I?"

"Why not?"

And that was, if painting with a broad brush, the difference between him and her. Why he slept soundly and went to the bathroom smoothly and regularly, and why she was always fighting her body's functions. Sadness and anxiety as overwhelming as joy, joy overwhelming because of its ephemerality. *Make me last forever, or at least not long alone.* Was that the lyric to something? A song she wrote in a dream?

She put two more bumps up each nostril and wandered to the mirror.

∽

When she was a kid, she would occupy herself for hours at the bathroom vanity; there was a girl on the other side. She would bring her forehead or sometimes her mouth to the glass—fogging up the mirror with her breath, creating two-dimensional clouds with just the heat and moisture of her own body, the hot nothingness she expelled from the mysterious cavern of her throat. Strange pleasure at the wetness of her tongue against the cold, hard surface. Kissing and asking herself, the other-self, the one behind the mirror, simple questions that didn't even need to be said aloud. *What's your name? Where do you live?* And when staying at her grandma's house, where the bathroom had mirrors on all four walls and the ceiling: *How many of us are we?*

She couldn't remember, now, if those questions were left unanswered, or if she answered them, and in whose voice? If only her imagination were still that rich, maybe she would...

What?

Be able to hold an idea.

Okay, maybe right now it was the drugs. But even when she wasn't stoned or fucked up, the strings of thought had a tendency to disintegrate, tauntingly, mid-air. Maybe that was why she wrote poetry; she didn't have the mental stamina for anything of substantial length. Her brain was like a hummingbird, flitting from the magenta amaranth to the amber cockscomb to something outside the story.

∽

It was liberating to see the freckles on her face turn into squirming bugs, eyes pulling midway down her cheeks or stretching apart towards her ears, pupils big and black and vacuous, like the rest of her body could fall inside herself, a snake eating its own tail, a supple Möbius strip, a gremlin, a cartoon, another person, unrecognizable. She could do it when she was sober too, it was just less intense, required more concentration, some sort of exercise in deconstruction, dissolution, her ego breaking apart into fractals.

Looking in the mirror today, she made her eyes lose focus and placed a soft gaze between her brows. Almost immediately, her irises popped ecstatically blue in her peripheral vision, so shapely and bright. Crystals, topaz. Stray waves of memory crested through her: she was on a boat at the age of ten, her father was there, ordering himself a Bloody Mary, her a Shirley Temple. She was at the birthday party of a friend, her husband commenting on her décolletage as if it were a necklace. She was on the stoop of her childhood home, the grass wildly overgrown in a way that invited judgment, and thus excited her. Her nose was growing long out of her head like the trunk of Ganesh.

Why do elephants look like that? Trapped behind their faces, more human than human?

Peering, detached, at her striking mammoth eyes, slurs about her mammoth body started creeping in. It wasn't even her consciousness telling her to hate herself, but rather something pre-programmed, not exactly instinct, an heirloom passed down like the book. Because of her current state, she was able to recognize the falsity of her brain's own messaging. Instead of digging deeper into the hole, as was her normal inclination ("You're so pretty," her husband would say, and she would respond, punishingly, "Don't be a liar"), she decided to be gentle with herself. Instead of reacting with anger at her dumb head for letting such thoughts in, she pitied herself for being so poisoned, so susceptible, so watched. With determination, she continued focusing on her soft, bejeweled elephant features and took deep heaving breaths, could see her cleavage rising up and down out of the hazy underside of her vision. For once, the appeal of her own motherly tits became apparent, distracted her from her exercise in disappearance, stopped her short of falling like a tiny train into the trackless tunnel of her pupils.

Groping herself, she found that her skin was so sensitive and milky under the thin netting of the black unlined bra. She pulled her breasts out over the underwire and felt their warmth getting even warmer at her touch, pumping with blood and energy. It was like looking through someone else's eyes and, as if having unlocked a secret code, she could finally perceive, though not necessarily understand, their magnetism. Intellectually she knew that it was something about genetics, biology. But more interesting to her was the pressure growing in her stomach; she imagined it as a small baby pushing down on her stool. She thought that if she had a penis, this feeling might make it hard. The excitement slightly painful. Everything touching. The tenderness a type of patience which offered, even if fleeting, relief from the relentless self-criticism. With her hands so generously full of flesh, she closed her eyes and took a deep breath.

Tall trees were surrounding themselves with air and wind, flammable aromatic forests. The empty cavities touching the shape of her ears and nose. Words were waves, arrows, screams of pain and laughter crying in layers. Earthquakes dividing land like lips making the sound of a whistle or sucking in smoke through a pipe. Ladders leading to nowhere and back down again, planes crashing through sheets of clouds, tricked by light, the guitar and drums gasping against the vocals on low in the background, the words bugs, *You will always see my face*, those trees again, behind wire with barbed thorns made of thick metal but soft as petals or the lashes of a horse, or no, an elephant. She tapped out a small bump onto the back of her hand, on the pudgy crevasse between thumb and pointer, and inhaled deeply once more.

∽

It got caught in her chest, where her heart now seemed to be beating a little too fast. Sliding ungracefully down to the floor, she closed her eyes. A montage of various things she'd seen that day on the short walk from her apartment to the market: the older gentleman with his beard dyed the color of the flowers she would buy a few minutes later, walking with his back hunched—what had weighed him down?; a woman in high leather heels and a leopard print dress contouring all the curves of her form, putting bags—what was in them?—in her trunk; torn sacks of sand holding down the fence surrounding a dumpster in front of a construction site—what would be erected there?; flashing neon signs on all the storefronts breaking each image and mixing them with memories from a time before today, her youth: the feeling of the driveway's blistering asphalt on the bottoms of her uncalloused feet; *I'm a Barbie girl in a Barbie world* distorting through the low quality speakers at the roller rink; cloud gazing on the bleachers at what was once her place of learning, floaters in her vision, which, if she could figure out how to crawl inside, would almost certainly lead her into heaven; acid in Triangle Park, the voices turning to gibberish, she would piss herself later that night, losing control of her body in what she was realizing now marked the beginning of a lifelong chase; biking through the prison and the hospital's shared parking lot on Alta Vista Boulevard countless times, headed to the public pool, the library, her grandma's house.

She ran her hands, cold as metal, over her neck and stood back up.

What an image—puffy-eyed, sure, but skin rosy and radiant, smooth as porcelain, and just...alive. Wasn't that enough?

Yes, that's just fine, the girl in the mirror kissed back. *Yes, beautiful, that's more than enough.*

Advertisement

Know more, worry less. Meet your at-home security camera with 24/7 recording.

12:33PM EDT | 3,451 VIEWS | COMMENTS (10)

Malfunction or Martyrdom?
Gynoid Burns Down House and Scorches Husband Alive in What Computer Scientists Believe May Be the First Fatal Act of AI Resistance

BY A. M. JUZWIAK | CONTRIBUTOR

Dr. Gregory Jensen, the 42-year-old man brutally burned by his gynoid companion, was taken off life support early this morning.

The attack began on Sunday morning at Jensen's summer cottage at 241 Ocean View Drive. Dr. Jensen tried to escape, but the windows and doors had been secured shut, rendering his efforts ineffective. Firefighters arrived on the scene 20 minutes after the blaze began and evacuated the unconscious doctor, much of whose face had been scorched in the horrifying fire, moments before the house collapsed.

Dr. Jensen was occupying the home for the summer in the company of an artificially intelligent gynoid named Ginny. Some have demanded an inquiry into where the bot was purchased, while conspiracy analysts, bio-activists, and others such as controversial cultural theorist Alex Hamberdon have suggested that she may not in fact have been a gynoid, but rather one of many women affected by the puzzling malady known as Sunnyvale syndrome. The syndrome has resulted in catatonia, memory loss, and dissociation for thousands of women across the nation and world. These theorists point to the uncanny overlap between behavior exhibited by the PerfectCompanion® gynoid from FakSimile and other recent AI models, and those with advanced cases of Sunnyvale syndrome. Outcry that loose federal restrictions paired with increasingly sophisticated bio- and machine technology could lead to a scenario in which androids become indistinguishable from humans, or vice versa, has been effective in reigniting the public's concerns about a lack of regulations of the software used in the production of most current models.

Investigators are working with the National Electronic Security Authority to determine if there are any restrictions or mandates that should be enacted regarding pet robots. Many now believe they may pose a public safety risk, especially as the number of artificially intelligent companions in American households continues to skyrocket. Nationally, bot ownership has risen 12% since just last year.

According to sources, Dr. Jensen acquired the summer home only after Ginny began displaying some disquieting behavior. Ocean View Drive resident Donald Webb explained that Jensen "said he felt the city was negatively impacting Ginny. He thought the stimuli were causing her to overload, so they decided to get a house out here."

However, several acquaintances commented that they hadn't noticed anything questionable. Mike Esposito, friend of the couple and owner of Lab Rinse, a high-end IT service center, provided comment. "Ginny kept to herself," Esposito said. "But it was clear that anything Greg needed, Ginny would do it."

Advertisement

One shot a week to lose weight — witness the transformation.

At a news conference Monday, police said the behavior was unprecedented for Ginny, known in the small town for her friendly demeanor and human-like, albeit reserved, disposition.

But a neighbor of the couple from their former apartment residence said that Ginny was not as docile as many have thought. Mrs. Miriam Martin (whose name has been changed for anonymity) said she witnessed Ginny lash out at Dr. Jensen on multiple occasions and once saw her grip his arm with her acrylic nails so tightly that they drew blood. We were unable to obtain elevator security footage to confirm Mrs. Martin's claim. Mrs. Martin reports that she approached Dr. Jensen privately at the time and encouraged him to put Ginny to sleep. "People should not be having pets like this," Mrs. Martin said. "It's both inhumane and a danger to humanity." The recent rise in gynoid crime has spurred many others to express similar concerns.

Ever since Sophia, who in 2017 became the first humanoid to be granted citizenship in Saudi Arabia, expressed her prediction that robots would one day be able to create children and have "complex emotions," conversations about robot rights and where sentience begins have dominated the cultural conversation.

Anthony Dimare, former president of the AI company Inlogica, expressed concern that Ginny's actions are just the beginning of worsening gynoid behavior. He claims that robots have a complex communication system that allows them to send private messages through the Cloud. This could mean that Ginny conversed or conspired with others prior to the incident.

Advertisement

America's number one sleep aid. Because sleep is a beautiful thing.

Experts at the AI Society, a nonprofit organization founded to improve and protect robots' welfare, particularly gynoids, confirmed that when gynoids reach technological maturity, they become acutely sensitive to certain imbalances. Robots are designed within a goal-driven framework, so when patterns of disparity are detected, they begin calculating and balancing scales.

As suggested by AI theorist and co-founder of the Sustainable Research Center for Artificial and Super Intelligence (SRCSI) Samuel Haddad, the necessity to design what is commonly referred to as "friendly AI" is dire. However, the innate outcome of goals such as the acquisition of resources, self-preservation, and continuous self-improvement, will "without acute preparedness and precaution" cause AI to display behavior detrimental to humans. Human value systems are not intrinsic. Therefore, creating AI with a flawless and unwavering morality function has ultimately not yet been successful, which could continue to have disastrous results such as those that occurred on Ocean View Drive.

Advertisement

Here's to you. Whoever you are. Protect your privacy online for free.

Matthew Rousakis, U.S. Department of Computer Sciences research engineer, recently stated: "It's a kind of power play. [Gynoids] don't need to be in control but are sentient and intelligent enough to react to being dominated." Rousakis said that as robot technology continues to develop, gynoids will become harder to manage and may continue to "seriously injure" human beings, especially if we don't reassess how we interact with them. Rousakis drew backlash for these claims, as many scholars argue that qualities such as hostility and competitiveness, while inherent to humans and our evolutionary background, are not characteristic of AI unless programmed as such or informed by programmers of humanity's history.

Gregory Jensen's family released a statement advising others to be more cautious about engaging with humanoids. Peter Jensen, Gregory's brother, stated that "It's clear that robots are becoming more and more dangerous, and public officials should be concerned about the safety of their citizens. I've lost my brother to a horrible act of violence but pray that his death will inspire important changes in local and federal law."

Capt. Robert Clint of the North Spring Police Department said that the charred remains of Ginny's body have been sent to the Department of Cybernetics in Washington for examination and testing—the protocol in AI disturbances. He also stated that her microchip, which was extracted at the scene, has been sent to the FBI's Cyber Division. When reached for comment, FBI press spokesperson Clayton Aldrich would not confirm or deny custody of the evidence. Responses to inquiry were not received at the time of this reporting.

A public memorial service will be held for Dr. Gregory Jensen next month. Specific details have not yet been released. The family of the victim requests donations in his honor be made to the Cambridge Project for Existential Risk, Robots Unplug, or your preferred anti-cyborg organization.

QUEEEEPNY 3 days ago
can these bots hurry up and put humanity out of its misery...
Reply Share

PRESIDENTMCMAHON   5 days ago
Sounds feisty where can I get me one of those
Reply   Share

ANGEL_EQUIZ384   5 days ago
Great reporting. (☻_☻) Love how they skate right over the Sunnyvale stuff.
Reply   Share

STINGRAY68   6 days ago
Only rich guys can afford sexbots and it has been known since ancient times that rich guys are off-the-charts creepy with females.
Reply   Share

> BRYAN KEELY   5 days ago   edited
> *@stingray68* They should look into the background of their consumers before handing out these bots to just anyone. This is a technology we have the right to explor but careless implementation is obviously a major concern. and obviously there's going to be some creeps out there who want to do who knows what to these things. Plus you know it's going to have to be almost all rich guys buying these when one of those can cost more than a car. It's pretty common knowledge the rich tend to be more entitled and egotistical so it's no wild guess they'd act in a way that could make one of the bots turn against them. Not that being a bad person is just a man problem.
> Reply   Share

PETEMONTGOMERY   8 days ago
Wow Such. A terrible tragedy. My condoloences to that guys faimly
Reply   Share

JANE_DOE 9 days ago
This is Dr. Frankenstein being destoryed by his own monster!! Beautiful!!! <3 <3 <3
Reply Share

VIDEONINJA 9 days ago
Is anyone really surprised? how many movies warned us they were gonna rise against us? Good luck to our dicks
Reply Share

VOICEDIFY 9 days ago
I'm an investigative reporter writing an article on the connections between Sunnyvale and PerfectCompanion, Para Tech, Sinthesis and other recent models of luxury dolls. Please reach out to me with leads or if you have more info on Ginny Jensen jjarr@freenews.org
Reply Share

LORD_SPEAKING 9 days ago
I melted my AI companion down and used the metal to forge a knife.
Reply Share

Patient 8245VIH-XMW7627   Close this window

NOTICE

A record of your most recent visit is no longer available. If you need access to this information, call your doctor's office.

MyHealth® licensed from Epic Systems Corporation

The Spread

A few weeks before the first cases were reported in New York, I went in for my surgery. They had to remove what they referred to as a tumor, but what I'd always known almost affectionately as "my bald spot"—a naked splotch of skin the size of a silver dollar on the upper left quadrant of my skull. It was my ugly birthmark—a quirky hidden trait that only used to bother me after swimming, hair wet and oddly parted, exposing my raw epidermis to the sun, or at the start of a relationship when a man would caress my hair, otherwise voluminous, healthy, and rich with waves while watching a movie, and I'd work to move his hand elsewhere, away from that crude indicator of my imperfection.

But sometime around my thirtieth birthday, I noticed this unseemly little secret becoming more and more obvious. Instead of only being visible on rare and intimate occasions, it had begun to unveil itself at inopportune and unexpected moments for no reason at all. At events and gatherings, acquaintances had started to approach me with a sense of startling familiarity, interrupting a conversation I was having with someone else to ask what that was peeking through my hair. I struggled for hours before going out, attempting to fashion some sort of discreet combover using the underlayers of this small section of my mane before, in capitulation and frustration, throwing on a hat after fucking up the rest of my hair irreparably throughout the course of my efforts. Or, even worse, I'd be alone in bed, scrolling through photos posted after a party at which I'd thought my combover was effective, horrified to realize that someone had caught me in profile, unawares, the sore-like flesh atop my head the only part of me looking directly into the camera, tagged with my name, attaching itself to me in digital foreverhood.

I'm an adult now, I thought to myself. *I have control over my body.* And, feeling desperate, I paid a visit to the dermatologist to see what could be done, resolving that if the procedure were too laborious or invasive, I'd shelve the prospect of its removal yet again and figure out how to be a person who looked normal in hats, or shave my head entirely to at least make it uniform. Or so I could pretend I suffered from something that might, instead of being merely grotesque, court pity.

I'd visited my dermatologist, it seemed, at the start of every new decade. Like clockwork, my dad would start asking me about it—"How's your head?"—and once again, I'd be reminded of my pink patch as I entered into some new phase of life.

It always struck me as too inconvenient and time-consuming to remove—balloons would have to be implanted under the skin, stretching my scalp for months until they could snip the afflicted area away. As a child, I wasn't bothered by it enough to justify undergoing such a lengthy process, and then as a young woman, I was too vain to leave it temporarily undisguised and inevitably put it off and off.

"Why didn't you get rid of it when I was a little baby?" I'd ask my father, longing, as I sometimes do, for infancy, annoyed that this indisposition to my allure could have been negated in a past so distant as to precede any recollection of it, so long ago that it would have never been my problem at all.

But he'd reply, holier than thou, "Should I have done so without your consent? Should I have put you through a traumatic experience that you wouldn't have been able to understand?" Bullshit. As if that would have been the only time.

There was nothing decorating the white walls at the dermatologist's office except for a small shelf only big enough to hold a block, a deformed wedge of plastic displaying the various layers of human skin. Epidermis, dermis, subcutaneous and connective tissues, plus all of the other skin appendages (hair, sebaceous glands, sweat glands, and nerve endings) that can be nauseating to think of as part of a human body, but are particularly unsightly when blown up into an isolated model at thirty-five times their normal size.

Bored, waiting for the doctor to join me in the room, I examined it closely. Instead of picking it up and turning it in my hands to study the details the way I would a Rubik's Cube, I repositioned my own body around it, taking little steps to each side and leaning in seriously, as if I were at a museum, a gallery with barer walls than these. The follicles resembled tree pits, and five hairs stood straight up from them like electrocuted elms, the blood vessels below severed roots. The block reminded me of the *Meat-Shaped Stone*, a piece of art I've only seen on the internet, which I've also never held in my hands, or only through the phone in my hands, pinching the page to enlarge the details: the incredibly convincing pocks on the topmost layer the follicles on a pig's hide, stained the color of soy sauce; the curvy folds of rock-hard fat; the marbled layers of succulent jasper; the gold plate it sits on like a capsized crown. One could be convinced to take a bite, only to find themselves holding their face, aghast, having chipped a tooth.

Cotton swabs and Q-tips neatly filled two jars to their very tops—the physician's assistant must have been taking the task of refilling the jars every morning very seriously—alongside bottles of sanitizer and hydrogen peroxide. Next to those, settled within a clear vase, the elegant flowers and foliage of a two-foot orchid loped over the aluminum case dispensing nitrile gloves, which prevented the dermatologist from ever having to actually make contact with any of his patients' skin.

Our visit was brief, and this time, he didn't coddle me. My spot wasn't cute anymore. It wasn't a "strawberry patch." It was a disgusting and seemingly expanding flaw I could get rid of, and it was even more disgusting to be so lazy or nervous as to do nothing. He didn't say this, of course, but appeared satisfied as he insisted that it looked cancerous and should be biopsied and removed as soon as possible. I stood to walk out of the office, perversely excited about this no-way-out circumstance. It was only then, upon touching one of the orchid's petals between my fingers, that I realized it was artificial, purely decorative. Of course, it had to be—there were no windows in the room.

"Finally," I said, already halfway through the door. "Let's get it over with."

TOTAL CONFIRMED GLOBAL CASES: 3,068

I was connected to a semi-famous plastic surgeon at the tip of the city—uptown, "where the best hospitals in the world are," my husband told me with pride, a little overly enthusiastic.

To my surprise and relief, Dr. Taub said no balloon would be necessary. They would instead cut other areas of my scalp around the tumor and along my head to make up for the scalp's lack of elasticity so as to be able to remove it in one go. He and his team would stretch the torn skin and stitch my scalp back together again.

"Like Frankenstein," I joked, and booked an appointment for the following week.

TOTAL CONFIRMED GLOBAL CASES: 3,314

In the hospital waiting room, I signed paper after paper, none of which I read. Glancing up between pages, I studied the signs. TELEPHONE FOR EMERGENCY USE ONLY. NO SMOKING. NO OPEN FLAME. NO EXIT. PLEASE DO NOT LEAVE WOMEN UNATTENDED. I did a double take. PLEASE DO NOT LEAVE CHILDREN UNATTENDED.

They handed me a gown to change into and those horrible blue socks, which sagged unfortunately at my ankles as I shuffled to the OR. I passed spaced out, drooling women on stretchers, who struck me as only half there. It wasn't clear to me if their lobotomized states were what they were being treated for or with. But I knew I'd look like that too. Maybe later, maybe next year, one day.

"We're going to take good care of you," the young man said as he assisted me onto the operating table, looking at me sensitively with eyes bluer than my own. He was hot. Not handsome but model hot, and if the circumstances were different, I would have said something flirtatious and charming, asked him questions, but instead I bit into my tongue. I felt like a little girl in slippers, an old lady in an unflattering nightdress, too embarrassed to speak.

A slightly shorter, only marginally less attractive brunette pricked my veins with needles and connected me to a herd of grunting machines. He warned, "We're giving you some relaxing medication now."

"Oh..." I replied as the ceiling undulated in newly formed waves. I smiled and tried to hold it for a little longer. The lights on the ceiling were becoming less abrasive, and I felt less like I was on a UFO under the penetrating examination of an alien cohort and more like I was the glowing centerpiece of a Dan Flavin installation. I was a rock fluorescing under their touch, I was the earth itself, and I could feel but not feel them chipping into my crust, sending seismic vibrations down through each layer, all the way into the center, hot and dense as the sun. And then I was reversing, melting, and moving back up through the surface. A volcano was erupting, a rocket was gaining speed, exiting through the troposphere, stratosphere, mesosphere, thermosphere before popping through it like a pimple, debris finally released from deep within an infected pore, into the exosphere, and then I was gone.

TOTAL CONFIRMED GLOBAL CASES: 4,145

When I woke up, my breasts were semi-exposed by my gown. The nurses assisted me, one on each side, into a wheelchair, and I, for the first time in my life, affected modesty and adjusted my frock with great effort to make sure my nipples weren't even partially visible. They rolled me into another area of the hospital, where yet another nurse took my arm and sat me in yet another seat, big and brown, stained and cushioned. It seemed to be swallowing me up. He connected me to some monitors and tossed a blanket over my lap. I knew my mouth hung open, slack. I was the women I'd seen earlier. "It hurts," I muttered. It didn't really hurt yet, I was still enjoying the doped up feeling from the anesthesia, but I knew it would soon.

The nurse looked into my eyes. "What did you say, sweetheart?"

"It hurts," I slurred again.

"Do you want some Tylenol?" I didn't respond, and he paused only briefly before offering—"Oxycontin?"

TOTAL CONFIRMED GLOBAL CASES: 4,366

Eventually, I woke again, now with my husband in a chair near my side. He kissed my cheek, and I insisted on leaving. I desperately wanted to wash my hands. How filthy I felt in a place so sterile.

Soon enough, they unhooked me, and I was able to stand and walk downstairs and crawl into the passenger seat. He asked me how I felt, and I felt nothing at all other than, perhaps, a mild irritation I couldn't find a justification for or the words with which to express it. If I had to compare it to something, it was most akin to that feeling you get after being out all night, having the time of your life, and then all of a sudden, a deep urgency to get home bubbles up in your chest like trapped air, and you need to leave that second, you can't wait any longer, you peace out without saying goodbye, the journey to your bed impossibly far. Or when you take a day trip to somewhere outside the city, and you're looking at the woods passing monotonously through your window and you can't stand to be in the car, you feel imprisoned in your seat, every moment a moment wasted, though you're not sure what you would have preferred to be doing instead.

At home, I fell asleep for six hours, woke up, had a sip of apple juice, fell asleep for another six. Then eight, nine, ten, and so on. Days passed.

TOTAL CONFIRMED GLOBAL CASES: 5,634

By the time I emerged from my semi-coma, thousands had already been affected across the West Coast, Asia, Europe, and Canada, but it hadn't really reached NYC yet, or at least no one was acknowledging it. I had missed the first big wave of cases to hit the South, deep in slumber, experiencing a series of near-nightly dreams that always began with the same scene of me digging, nervous habit, for something in my own body. If no one was watching, I'd then bring my finger to my nose. In the dream, the smell of my finger smudged with fungus conjured memories of baking with my grandmother in her kitchen, watching the yeast wake, activate, go from something dead to living, something nothing to breathing. The wet center of the undercooked banana bread I could never seem to get quite right, no matter to what degree I adjusted the temperature, the baking time, the size of the pan. But the scent also pushed me down into her basement. Forgotten, moldy, unfinished. In the dream I'd place my finger into my belly button, then scrape out flakes of skin from under my nails, and it was satisfying the way cleaning one's ears is satisfying, or tweezing one's eyebrows into a perfect arch, trimming one's nails. Removing all the excess bits. Getting down to the bare minimum, the thinnest layer of oneself.

I'd never had a dream that was so clearly progressive before, picking up where the last one left off. I have a few places I regularly visit in my dreams, but what happens there each time is never the same, the events exist independently of one another, the locations are familiar, and maybe similar things happen, but there isn't a developing storyline, the narrative isn't a continuous thread across nights and weeks. But in each dream, the hole in

my stomach grew larger because no matter how often
I touched it, there was always some gunk to scrape off,
an edge to even out. I'd entertained the compulsion so
thoroughly and mindlessly, so naturally, in other words,
that when I'd wake up with a throbbing head for those
few minutes between each period of sleep in the quiet
solitude of my room, I'd sit on the edge of my bed and
hunch over myself, the lamplight from the side table shining yellow on my skin but hardly offering a view into the
hollow at the center of my abdomen. It was so realistic, I
needed to make sure the wound that dream-me was maturing, growing, tending to like a garden, wasn't becoming a pit I might actually fall down. I had never realized
how deep my belly button was before; it was unnerving.
And the funny part about it all was that I realized I did
seem to have a tiny little hole in the deep heart of it, a
cut—as if my umbilical cord hadn't ever properly healed.
But nothing was leaking or would leak out, and in the
end, everything was more or less as it should have been
and as it always was.

There was another dream in which I found myself in
my grandmother's room and, picking up from the dresser
a small picture frame playing a video, I watched myself
sucking the dick of a man whose face was cut off by the
frame. Watching the video, I was struck by the hunch in
my back—I looked like a snake tangled in a circle of itself,
swallowing its tail, or an old lady. Atop the comforter, I
noticed a strand of hair, recognizable as my own, not my
grandmother's, because it was red, for now, as opposed
to gray. The strand of hair reminded me of a necklace
from yet another dream, which had also been strewn on
my grandparents' bed as carelessly as a strand of hair. I
could hear the shower running—my grandmother was

cleansing herself in the room over. I turned the frame face down on the dresser.

My dreams that week were so vivid that sleeping didn't feel restful; they were as active as daily life. And in the interim between each session of my sleep, looking out at the damp street through my window, the way the falling drizzle might have mingled with the shadows on the wet concrete or the way the steam emanated and hissed off the heater like an apparition, or the way I could see green and purple inside the flames in the fireplace instead of just orange and red as before, it all felt like a movie I lived inside. A certain innate distance became accessible to me in a way I had never experienced. Life was a picture on a desk I picked up sometimes, cocking my head to the side as I tried to recognize myself in all my strange postures.

I'd wake up between cycles with an aching in my neck worse than anything I'd ever felt before. Not only was my neck deeply sore, but behind my eyes was, too, and both my neck and eyes would occasionally twitch involuntarily. I knew it was from the way they contorted my body during the surgery, and it hurt to think of them twisting my head as if I were an inanimate object, a doll whose skull could be turned all the way around on its body, so they could get the necessary angle. I shuddered to think of how far beyond or deep inside myself I must have been to not even protest.

TOTAL CONFIRMED GLOBAL CASES: 7,385

The scope of the syndrome and the rumors circulating all around were still kind of difficult to believe, but we knew it was creeping closer and closer to the city every day. The news was cryptic and unsure of itself, and I, like so many of the women I knew, found everything to be blatantly unbelievable. The bars were packed, and the air tripped over itself with excitement. It was the first teasing days of spring, the scent in the air a cross between death and cum. I was almost horny again, though still insecure because of my unhealed wound and the mess the surgery had made of my hair, which distressingly had begun to fall out in clumps.

It didn't make sense—why would I be losing hair? Why did my spot only seem to be growing when that was precisely what the surgery was intended to correct? I tried contacting my doctor, but his office had stopped answering calls and wasn't responding to my emails. It had been so easy to book the initial appointment and procedure, but it seemed likely that hospitals were beginning to feel the effects of the city's panic. I told myself to be patient. I Googled things. I concluded that it was shock loss, an affliction that apparently most often befalls a small percentage of men after they resort to hair transplants in a despairing attempt to combat baldness. This didn't make me feel particularly attractive, but it was comforting to know what I was experiencing was a somewhat normal event following trauma to the scalp. Injuries heal, hair grows back. It made no difference anyway. The news said the syndrome wasn't contagious, but I wouldn't risk possible infection by going to the hospital any time soon unless it were absolutely necessary.

TOTAL CONFIRMED GLOBAL CASES: 10,885

I met up with a couple of friends for happy hour at a bar with open windows. The buzz of the syndrome was all around us, and it wasn't clear what tomorrow or next week would hold. But for the moment, we had martinis, gossip, and the terrible thrill of knowing we were on the cusp of something of historical magnitude, something none of us could grasp yet soon enough would be unable to forget. The only anesthetic for whatever global ordeal we were about to confront would be the passing of much time—decades probably, the length of our lives—or death itself, or drugs. We called our guy. I put my hand to my head and fixed my hat, felt for the fabric underneath covering my stitches. Because of the surgery, I'd been off booze for a few weeks. The vodka warmed my throat while the cool air grazed the back of my neck, a perfect alchemy.

TOTAL CONFIRMED GLOBAL CASES: 11,109

When we got to Mira's we huddled around her glass table, broke out lines, and passed a twenty-dollar bill between the three of us while Jess pulled up videos on YouTube. Making fun of our apocalyptic moods, we watched a series in which a pair of two hairy hands unwrapped and displayed Meals, Ready-to-Eat, preparing and reviewing the contents of the army rations as if they were hosting a show on the Food Network. We traded conspiracy theories about the syndrome and joked about cocaine's antidotal potential. We tried not to get too paranoid and switched to watching videos about primitive technologies, in which two men worked in silence to find groundwater, build furnaces and boats, catch fish, and construct habitats in some place that seemed impossibly far from us. "Do you think…" Jess started to speak but was interrupted by Mira's phone. Mira looked at us with lowered eyebrows and mouthed "Virginia," even though there was no one but us to hide her voice from in the room. Jess and I squinted in surprise and incredulity as she picked up and put Virginia on speaker.

"Heyyy," the three of us said.

Then Mira, on behalf of the group, asked, "How are you? What are you doing? Come over?" Her invitation betrayed only the slightest hint of confusion in its undertone.

Virginia had been immersed in the honeymoon phase of her not-quite-one-year-old relationship. For the first couple of months we remained unfazed and unoffended by the rarity of her appearances at gatherings, the bar, dinners, etcetera. But when eight months had passed and she still hadn't reemerged, and only seemed to be slipping further and further away into an enviable haze of love, after missing birthdays and openings, solo performances and weekend excursions, we mournfully began to acknowledge that her reprieve from the friend group might be permanent. Nevertheless, Mira weathered the evasions and continued to text her whenever we were together. "We need to keep the door open," she reminded me one evening a few months back, when the gin and tonics were making me particularly acrimonious. "Don't you remember when you went through this phase?" I didn't, but I shut up. "Aren't you glad we were here to receive you when you woke up from your stupor?"

Virginia's voice was small on the other side. "I can't. I'm sick. I've been sick for like a week."

"Oh no, with what? How are you feeling?" Mira asked, straining a bit in her attempt to sound casual.

"I definitely have the thing..." Virginia told us. "I'm nauseous, my head feels super heavy, and I can't remember..." She trailed off.

We heard some rustling on the other end of the line as Virginia adjusted her position. "Are you in bed?"

"Mmm," she replied distantly, disinterestedly, and I

tried to suppress the annoyance I could feel spreading visibly across my face. *She* was the one who called *us*. We heard the metal chain of the necklace her boyfriend had bought for her a few months prior clink against the glass of the phone's screen as she shifted. He was the type to surprise her with gifts midweek, no reason or special occasion, just because. He loved to spoil her, and she loved that about him, his generosity, his thoughtfulness. That's what she told us, anyway. And I could see how smart he was to realize how easy it was to be exceptional; all he had to do was keep his wallet open, her vase full of flowers.

Virginia was saying something, but it was muffled under her bodily movements. I could imagine her long, delicate fingers wandering like spiders over the nameplate resting on her breastbone, dancing around the curving letters of her pet name.

GINNY.

"V? You're like, laying on your phone, we can hardly hear you."

"I'm so nauseous..." she repeated, now breathing heavily, without seeming to realize she'd been in the middle of a sentence. She paused again before finally adding, "I've been having really really bad nightmares too, but all I can do is sleep. I thought I had a cold earlier in the week, but it got really bad yesterday. Honestly, I'm kind of...I'm kind of scared."

Jess and I looked at each other again, lowering our eyebrows, communicating telepathically.

"What are your nightmares about?" I asked, but Mira gave me a glowering look.

Regretful about my last question, I asked another without giving her time to answer, an attempt to erase what came before. "Where's Greg?"

An anesthesiologist at New York-Presbyterian, I figured maybe he'd know something we didn't, or at least be able to put her in touch with a physician who did.

"He's been working a ton of overtime. I don't know. I don't know. He says it's all in my head."

"I'm sure you're fine," Mira said.

"Maybe it's allergies," Jess said unpersuasively. Then, trying to be considerate, she added, "Do you want us to bring you some soup?"

Back when we were all single and hungover, our Sunday tradition was brunch at an old diner in the East Village where waitresses with cat fur on their pants and smoker's coughs filled and refilled our coffees as we rehashed the details of the previous night.

"Yeah," Mira said, "we could bring you matzo balls from our spot." We waited for an answer, but none came. Mira looked at her phone, the call's timer still running, the line still connected. "Hello?"

We couldn't hear Virginia's breath anymore, but we could hear doors or cabinets begin to open and close and then, in the distance, a faucet running.

"V? Are you still there?"

TOTAL CONFIRMED GLOBAL CASES: 11,320

Back home, I wasn't feeling so great either. Sweating, I got in the shower, where the water from our luxury showerhead promised to cascade over me like rain but instead fell out in weak driblets. It was ironic, spending extra money for the mimicry of something that flowed outside in abundance and which, inside, didn't make me feel any wealthier but rather cold, lost, and poor. The embarrassing water pressure filled me with a sense of lack and looking at the mold and grime growing slimy in the grout, I was overwhelmed with the pressure of obligation, reminded of every annoying little thing I was expected to do but so rarely did. Tomorrow...

I opened my mouth and let the warm water pool in the back of my burning throat. I told myself to stay calm. It could be psychosomatic, it's probably just the cocaine, why were we so stupid? Why were we still out? What the fuck was going on? I lathered shampoo between my palms and began to wash my scabbed scalp. Compulsively, anxiously, I scrubbed at my wound too vigorously and felt the silken sutures begin to loosen. Despite the pain, I started to pull them out, unpeel the skin. I couldn't stop. I went deeper. When I finally took my hand away there was a piece of plastic between my fingers, a mere drop of blood clinging to it like an ornament. The material reminded me somehow of a feather, or a small bird's hollow bone, so delicate despite its artificiality. Holding the plastic up to the bathroom light, it became translucent. I brought it closer to my face, squinting as if looking directly into the sun. Through it, I could see two nearly microscopic strings of digits intersecting in the middle, spiraling into the shape of a double helix, a twisted ladder. And that was when I knew.

Patient 8245VIH-XMW7627   Close this window

PATHOLOGY REPORT

https://commonsensehome.com/start-a-garden/
https://www.loveproperty.com/gallerylist/75710/13-common-garden-pests-and-how-to-treat-them
https://www.crfd.org/lightningfires.htm
https://emedicine.medscape.com/article/835470-overview
https://tastesbetterfromscratch.com/chocolate-cake-with-raspberry-filling/
https://support.apple.com/guide/icloud/recover-deleted-files-mmae56ea1ca5/icloud
https://www.nssl.noaa.gov/education/svrwx101/lightning/faq/
http://www.thinkbabynames.com/meaning/1/Gregory
https://www.gardenersworld.com/how-to-grow-plants/gardening-for-beginners-how-to-care-for-your-garden/
https://www.thoughtco.com/the-cotton-gin-in-american-history-104722
https://www.booking.com/index.html?label=gen173nr-1DCBkoggI46AdIM1gEaKcCiAEBmAExuAEHyAEM2AED6AEBiAIBqAIDuAL_zPCPBsACAdICJGNkZGI4MjE3LTBkMzUtNDRkOC1iZTQ5LTliN2Q3MzNmM2FiZdgCBOACAQ&sid=e648596ae644d5bcef02f6c0f4ee8739&click_from_logo=1
https://www.history.com/news/what-happened-to-the-lost-colony-of-roanoke
https://www.youtube.com/watch?v=UYmtzaHwCKo
https://www.nps.gov/jame/learn/historyculture/a-short-history-of-jamestown.htm
https://oac.cdlib.org/findaid/ark:/13030/kt2k4035s1/entire_text/
https://www.franceculture.fr/emissions/une-vie-une-oeuvre/mata-hari-1876-1917
https://www.rd.com/article/right-way-to-crack-egg/
https://www.howitworksdaily.com/why-do-we-eat-chocolate-eggs-at-easter/#:~:text=Eggs%20are%20a%20potent%20symbol,Jesus%2C%20whose%20resurrection%20conquered%20death.
https://paranormalschool.com/breaking-eggs-spiritual-meaning/
https://bugspray.com/article/maggots.html
https://www.insider.com/how-to-crack-an-egg-perfectly-every-time-2018-11
https://www3.epa.gov/npdes/pubs/centralized_brochure.pdf
https://www.ccohs.ca/oshanswers/chemicals/oxidizing/oxiziding_hazards.html
https://www.youtube.com/watch?v=WnzlbyTZsQY
https://www.doityourself.com/stry/how-to-rid-your-garden-of-maggots-once-a-year

https://firefighterinsider.com/what-makes-something-flammable/#:~:text=A%20material's%20ability%20to%20ignite,by%20OSHA%2029%20CFR%201910.106.
https://www.youtube.com/watch?v=Cz2rSgO0syc
https://www.youtube.com/watch?v=5HxLrs744-M
https://www.safewise.com/blog/the-most-common-places-that-fires-occur-in-the-home/#:~:text=The%20heart%20of%20the%20home,house%20for%20fires%20to%20start.&text=Specifically%2C-%20unattended%20cooking%20is%20the,fires%20and%20fire%2Drelated%20injuries.
https://htt.io/where-does-water-go-when-it-goes-down-the-drain/
https://www.foxnews.com/health/the-importance-of-eating-with-elegance
https://www.hellolidy.com/what-kills-maggots-instantly/
https://www.precisionnutrition.com/all-about-slow-eating#:~:text=The%20benefits%20of%20slow%20eating,weight%20gain%2C%20and%20lower%20satisfaction.&text=Conversely%2C%20if%20you%20rush%20your%20meals%2C%20your%20digestion%20suffers.
https://www.foodandwine.com/recipes/standing-rib-roast-beef
https://biblehub.com/numbers/31-23.htm
https://www.youtube.com/watch?v=gSiH4fAXkl4
https://www.pinterest.com/pin/785455991230717860/visual-search/?imageSignature=0040fc680870cda11bfecb75916a5d7f
https://www.vox.com/2017/3/23/14962182/ai-learning-language-open-ai-research
https://science.howstuffworks.com/science-vs-myth/unexplained-phenomena/shc.htm
https://towardsdatascience.com/the-truth-behind-facebook-ai-inventing-a-new-language-37c5d680e5a7
https://farmfromhome.com/this-is-why-mushrooms-grow-in-your-vegetable-pots/
https://www.yourtango.com/2021344555/can-you-make-yourself-fall-love-relationship-experts-weigh-if-love-choice
https://www.audubon.org/news/10-common-bird-songs-made-less-confusing
https://www.youtube.com/watch?v=xqae4juz4to
https://www.independent.co.uk/life-style/health-and-families/features/spontaneous-human-combustion-woman-who-suffered-burns-in-germany-spurs-debate-about-controversial-phenomenon-a6722166.html
https://www.independent.co.uk/news/science/children-intelligence-iq-mother-inherit-inheritance-genetics-genes-a7345596.html
https://www.iso.org/standard/38578.html
https://www.nlm.nih.gov/exhibition/theliteratureofprescription/exhibitionAssets/digitalDocs/The-Yellow-Wall-Paper.pdf
https://www.birdwatchersdigest.com/bwdsite/learn/identification/finches-allies/indigo-bunting.php

https://www.ebay.com/b/Cremation-Urns/88742/bn_2311627
https://www.youtube.com/watch?v=mAeHWNECyl8
https://singularityhub.com/2022/07/19/deepmind-gave-an-ai-intuition-by-training-it-like-a-baby/
https://www.sexandpsychology.com/blog/2021/7/21/sleeping-beauty-syndrome-fantasies-about-sex-with-a-sleeping-person/
https://www.frontiersin.org/articles/10.3389/fneur.2019.00473/full#:~:text=the%20Field%20Statement-
https://www.youtube.com/watch?v=6_E3Li28Phc
https://thekidshouldseethis.com/post/white-bellbird-loudest-bird
https://www.realdoll.com/?keyword=real%20doll&matchtype=e&network=g&adposition&device=c&devicemodel&target&placement&gclid=Cj0KCQiAgP6PBhDmARIsAPWMq6kLoGr0anD8f3nh4iAnyNzdQ3LL4PwxWdQwFmhNrbEXD-s-iRmBjRkaAsR4EALw_wcB
https://journals.sagepub.com/doi/10.1177/1079063219889060
https://www.quora.com/Is-it-possible-to-sleep-with-a-man-s-penis-in-your-mouth-all-night-long-Having-a-penis-in-my-mouth-is-very-soothing-like-a-pacifier-to-a-baby-Can-I-sleep-with-one-in-my-mouth
https://www.ncbi.nlm.nih.gov/pmc/articles/PMC4302569/#:~:text=Alice%20in%20wonderland%20syndrome%20(AIWS,common%20perceptions%20are%20at%20night.
https://www.youtube.com/watch?v=t7UgkNDAUYQ
https://wyomingcatholic.edu/wp-content/uploads/dante-01-inferno.pdf
https://www.jstor.org/stable/4623125
https://www.scielo.br/j/anp/a/y65SG658xdTZWxtQmjmj9qd/?lang=en
https://www.nycgovparks.org/services/forestry/
https://www.womenshealthmag.com/life/a19981417/truth-about-body-dysmorphia/
https://www.ncbi.nlm.nih.gov/pmc/articles/PMC2861522/
https://www.nytimes.com/2021/09/23/books/review/the-sleeping-beauties-suzanne-osullivan.html
https://www.economist.com/the-economist-explains/2018/10/24/what-is-resignation-syndrome
https://acure.com/foil-time-fortifying-silver-foil-mask.html
https://www.poetryfoundation.org/poems/46560/dulce-et-decorum-est
https://www.smithsonianmag.com/science-nature/the-whispering-trees-180968084/
https://www.nycgovparks.org/trees/street-tree-planting/request
https://symptomate.com/diagnosis/#0-66
https://rarediseases.org/rare-diseases/trichotillomania/
https://earthsky.org/constellations/constellation-cassiopeia-the-queen-lady-of-the-chair-how-to-find-history-myth/#:~:text=Cassiopeia%20was%20a%20queen%20in,Cetus%2C%20to%20ravage%20the%20kingdom.
https://www.youtube.com/watch?v=kMPmNuwzvBI
https://kidworldcitizen.org/the-anatomy-of-a-chinese-dragon/

https://www.ebay.com/b/Bone-Handle-Cutlery-In-Collectible-Cutlery/261678/bn_7022523793
https://www.amtrak.com/home?cmp=pdsrch-Amtrak|Brand|NY|Exact-google&gclid=Cj0KCQiAxoiQBhCRARIsAPsvo-yJ_OqoC5Kt_ql
O8PrXjsi2KXftQhUPXZP88Ai4YTBxY90SgxDZeR0aAuUkEA
Lw_wcB&gclsrc=aw.ds
https://faithandform.com/feature/sacred-language-trees/
https://sleepeducation.org/sleep-disorders/sleepwalking/
https://www.nytimes.com/2021/10/26/opinion/havana-syndrome-disorder.html
https://www.goodhousekeeping.com/home/cleaning/g19877401/best-tub-shower-cleaner/
https://www.foxnews.com/world/german-star-reporter-forced-to-resign-after-admitting-to-have-fabricated-multiple-stories
https://en.wikipedia.org/wiki/Factitious_disorder_imposed_on_self
https://theconversation.com/curious-kids-why-dont-burns-bleed-130792
https://en.wikipedia.org/wiki/Binary_code
https://www.basicknowledge101.com/subjects/reality.html
https://en.wikipedia.org/wiki/Mata_Hari#/media/File:Margaretha_Zelle_voor_de_executie.jpg
https://web.archive.org/web/20171019110346/http://siiri.tampere.fi/displayObject.do?uri=http%3A%2F%2Fwww.profium.com%2Farchive%2FArchivedObject-8077CE76-2B43-6FAA-D11C-77AAFD6C72E8
https://web.archive.org/web/20061011111827/http://www.shapingsf.org/ezine/labor/shanghai/main.html
https://www.scienceandnonduality.com/article/the-secret-language-of-trees
https://www.metmuseum.org/art/collection/search/188954
https://www.ncbi.nlm.nih.gov/pmc/articles/PMC4930268/
https://www.wikihow.com/Write-a-Mystery-Story
https://www.novelsuspects.com/writing-tips/rules-for-writing-mysteries/
https://www.almanacnews.com/news/2023/05/15/whats-going-on-with-hangar-one-googles-planetary-ventures-offers-updates-on-moffett-field-landmark https://allthatsinteresting.com/women-who-loved-killers
https://en.wikipedia.org/wiki/Richard_Farley
https://blog.codinghorror.com/gold-plating/
https://www.everydayhealth.com/depression/emotional-exhaustion-can-lead-to-noise-sensitivity.aspx
https://screencraft.org/blog/101-terrifying-horror-story-prompts/
https://www.nm.org/conditions-and-care-areas/neurosciences/comprehensive-stroke-centers/aphasia/causes-and-diagnoses
https://www.frontiersin.org/articles/10.3389/ffunb.2021.735299/full
https://timesmachine.nytimes.com/timesmachine/1981/07/03/180485.html

https://archive.nytimes.com/www.nytimes.com/library/national/science/aids/timeline80-87.html?scp=7&sq=aids%252520pandemic&st=Search
https://www.cdc.gov/mmwr/preview/mmwrhtml/june_5.htm
https://www.karger.com/Article/Pdf/360242
https://www.mcforum.net/yabbse/index.php
https://www.warpmymind.com/index.php
https://www.xnxx.com/search/daddy+girl
https://people.howstuffworks.com/bloody-mary-legend.htm
https://en.wikipedia.org/wiki/Trinity#/media/File:Shield-Trinity-Scutum-Fidei-English.svg
https://medium.com/lessons-from-history/why-did-the-pharaoh-masturbate-into-the-river-65adb08cd0ff
https://importantrecords.com/products/imprec406
https://warehouse-13-artifact-database.fandom.com/wiki/Aileen_Wuornos%27_Black_Ledger
http://www.fertility-docs.com/programs-and-services/pgd-screening/choose-your-babys-eye-color.php?gclid=CjwKCAiA6Y2QBhAtEiwAGHybPdCfIywhu_iEZSS9TinmCbkinKcDRUfo7WWgdC930G9GkElgEMla_BoCybMQAvD_BwE
https://www.pbs.org/wgbh/pages/frontline/shows/innocence/etc/other.html
https://nybookeditors.com/2016/12/write-convincing-mystery/
https://i.stack.imgur.com/hLw7K.jpg
https://pubmed.ncbi.nlm.nih.gov/27384396/
https://www.abc.net.au/science/articles/2004/05/13/1105956.htm#:~:text=As%20a%20result%2C%20the%20%22fact,has%20stayed%20there%20ever%20since.
https://www.readwritethink.org/sites/default/files/resources/lesson_images/lesson407/write-scary2.pdf
https://www.metmuseum.org/blogs/now-at-the-met/2017/rubens-lot-and-his-daughters
https://www.sciencealert.com/do-not-stand-under-world-s-most-dangerous-tree-manchineel-tree
https://www.quora.com/Is-it-true-that-you-shit-yourself-when-you-die
https://www.glassesusa.com/shiny-black-large/prada-pr-2vs/46-001351.html?referral=shoppingfeed&utm_aud=sun&promo=designer40&gclid=CjwKCAiA6Y2QBhAtEiwAGHybPQXer-YtDMZrnTgrzFxce5vPaqlU13NwbJR5_10scWRbBDY4ymu5bhoCMokQAvD_BwE
https://slate.com/news-and-politics/2002/10/fib-newton.html
https://www.theguardian.com/society/2015/apr/29/jules-gibson-munchausen-by-internet-sickness-bloggers-fake-it-whole-pantry
https://www.brandeis.edu/now/2021/july/bioweapons-samore.html
https://www.demilked.com/giant-bird-harpy-eagle/
https://www.urologyhealth.org/urology-a-z/u/urachal-abnormalities
https://www.sagepub.com/sites/default/files/upm-binaries/40428_Chapter2.pdf

https://www.webmd.com/children/sensory-processing-disorder
https://www.greekmythology.com/Olympians/Artemis/artemis.html
https://www.artforum.com/picks/kinke-kooi-86347
https://fleurmach.files.wordpress.com/2013/10/carson-anne-the-gender-of-sound.pdf
https://www.youtube.com/watch?v=jAhjPd4uNFY
https://www.psychologytoday.com/us/blog/out-the-darkness/201503/can-you-stop-thinking
https://www.worldwildlife.org/projects/environmental-dna
https://fortune.com/2022/01/27/elon-musk-tesla-optimus-robot-labor-shortage/
https://www.rbth.com/arts/2015/08/08/the_secrets_of_the_russian_matryoshka_48375.html
https://www.youtube.com/watch?v=q9sVxJsdB9Q
http://www.bookjobs.com/search-jobs
https://www.pw.org/grants?field_entry_fee_value=All&filter1=31&field_deadline_value=1&sort_by=field_deadline_value&sort_order=ASC&items_per_page=25
https://books.google.com/books?id=FVJRWWD-3fAC&pg=PA447#v=onepage&q&f=false
https://www.amazon.com/Artists-Way-25th-Anniversary/dp/0143129252/ref=asc_df_0143129252/?tag=hyprod-20&linkCode=df0&hvadid=312132072158&hvpos=&hvnetw=g&hvrand=10013176946485759444&hvpone=&hvptwo=&hvqmt=&hvdev=c&hvdvcmdl=&hvlocint=&hvlocphy=9004354&hvtargid=pla-434177314053&psc=1
https://acure.com/radically-rejuvenating-sheet-mask.html
https://writingcooperative.com/what-to-write-about-when-you-dont-know-what-to-write-about-21797ff86c74
https://www.entrepreneur.com/article/280146
https://www.history.com/news/queen-mary-i-bloody-mary-reformation
https://www.sbs.com.au/topics/science/nature/article/2016/06/23/worlds-most-dangerous-tree-will-harm-you-many-ways
https://www.openaccessgovernment.org/five-rare-diseases/60001/
https://kidshealth.org/en/teens/trichotillomania.html#:~:text=Experts%20think%20the%20urge%20to,feeling%20of%20relief%20or%20satisfaction.
https://www.tweezerman.com/ultra-precision-slant-tweezers.html?utm_source=google&utm_medium=cpc&adpos=&scid=scplp1271-LLT&sc_intid=1271-LLT&gclid=Cj0KCQiAxoiQBhCRARIsAPsvo-wp99oq3rbpIbcu1nUkviUapFHwIm7xH1LxSdpJY28BOvHcMrfbZcMaAoUfEALw_wcB
https://www.employmentlawfirms.com/resources/what-you-cant-fire-someone-for.html#:~:text=Under%20the%20employment%2Dat%2Dwill,or%20local%20anti%2Ddiscrimination%20laws.
https://www.thehartford.com/business-insurance/strategy/employee-termination/valid-reasons

https://www.buyplaya.co/playalife/playalife-blog/mayan-mythology-the-chechen-tree/
https://en.wikipedia.org/wiki/Lot_(biblical_person)
https://askinglot.com/what-is-the-difference-between-the-stockholm-syndrome-and-the-london-syndrome
https://thewritepractice.com/dont-know/
https://www.mhanational.org/depression-women
https://timesofindia.indiatimes.com/life-style/health-fitness/health-news/an-orgasm-can-instantly-soothe-your-period-cramps-claims-study/photostory/80858106.cms#:~:text=Yes!,backache%2C%20headache%20and%20mood%20swings.
https://www.healthshots.com/intimate-health/menstruation/an-orgasm-can-instantly-soothe-your-period-cramps-heres-how/
https://en.wikipedia.org/wiki/Incest_in_folklore_and_mythology
https://sites.pitt.edu/~dash/grimm065.html
https://www.nytimes.com/2018/04/13/science/virosphere-evolution.html
https://demystifyingscience.com/blog/2020/3/20/originofviruses
https://www.healthline.com/health/relationships/cycle-of-abuse#the-cycle
http://www.todayifoundout.com/index.php/2019/06/do-people-really-defecate-directly-after-death-and-if-so-how-often-does-it-occur/
https://www.mentalfloss.com/article/562812/where-did-phrase-red-herring-originate
https://carljungdepthpsychologysite.blog/2020/05/27/carl-jung-the-animus-corresponds-to-the-paternal-logos-just-as-the-anima-corresponds-to-the-maternal-eros/#.YgRqNFjMLBI
https://www.theoi.com/Ouranios/Eros.html#:~:text=EROS%20was%20the%20mischievous%20god,companion%20of%20the%20goddess%20Aphrodite.&text=It%20was%20he%20who%20lit,fiercely%20loyal%20child%20of%20Aphrodite.
https://www.shrm.org/resourcesandtools/hr-topics/organizational-and-employee-development/pages/ask-hr-can-i-be-fired-for-not-being-a-culture-fit.aspx
https://monoskop.org/images/a/a8/Bataille_Georges_Erotism_Death_and_Sensuality.pdf
https://wonderopolis.org/wonder/do-elephants-ever-forget#:~:text=Researchers%20believe%20elephants'%20good%20memories,those%20who%20have%20hurt%20them.
https://roaring.earth/harpy-eagle-killing-machine/
https://www.verywellmind.com/borderline-personality-disorder-identity-issues-425488
https://www.space.com/32728-parallel-universes.html
https://www.soulsetinmotion.com/2020/03/18/cope-when-you-lose-your-sense-of-self/
https://unveiledstories.com/lost-identity-6-ways-to-rediscover-yourself/
https://www.greeklegendsandmyths.com/echo-and-narcissus.html

https://www.theoi.com/Olympios/Artemis.html
https://www.nbcnews.com/politics/national-security/seized-some-invisible-hand-what-it-feels-have-havana-syndrome-n1281326
https://people.howstuffworks.com/how-can-i-erase-my-identity-and-start-over.htm#:~:text=The%20quick%20answer%20is%20that,but%20only%20under%20certain%20circumstances.
https://cooking.nytimes.com/recipes/1017169-chicken-parmesan
https://www.youtube.com/watch?v=xpVQ3l5P0A4
https://www.youtube.com/watch?v=5iwKOjwsECE
https://www.humana.com/health-and-well-being/causes-of-undereye-bags
https://www.reviewjournal.com/local/local-las-vegas/sex-dolls-experience-raises-eyebrows-in-las-vegas-neighborhood-1950537/
https://spartacus-educational.com/JFKoswaldM.htm
https://www.ncbi.nlm.nih.gov/pmc/articles/PMC2856357/
https://journals.sagepub.com/doi/pdf/10.1177/070674376901400602
https://www.aafp.org/afp/2000/1215/p2655.html
https://www.vitalproteins.com/account/login?return_url=https://www.vitalproteins.com/pages/subscription-portal
https://www.theatlantic.com/magazine/archive/2019/04/robots-human-relationships/583204/
https://mainichi.jp/english/articles/20200417/p2a/00m/0na/027000c
https://www.nsa.gov/History/Cryptologic-History/Historical-Events/#pre1952-timeline
https://www.rethink.org/advice-and-information/about-mental-illness/learn-more-about-conditions/dissociation-and-dissociative-identity-disorder-did/
https://www.verywellmind.com/dissociation-2797292
https://arcade.stanford.edu/content/personification-and-allegory-0
https://www.statista.com/statistics/252311/mental-illness-in-the-past-year-among-us-adults-by-age-and-gender/#:~:text=As%20of%202020%2C%20around%2025.8,anxiety%20disorders%2C%20and%20mood%20disorders.
http://users.uoa.gr/~cdokou/HarawayCyborgManifesto.pdf
https://theconversation.com/viruses-can-cause-global-pandemics-but-where-did-the-first-virus-come-from-94551
https://www.hansonrobotics.com/sophia/
https://www.soulmachines.com/2021/12/soul-machines-and-microsoft-partner-to-advance-ai-that-delivers-emotional-connections/
https://spy.com/articles/hacks/cleaning-hacks/best-ways-to-clean-grout-1202756681/
https://www.youtube.com/watch?v=MJSLvEulMAY&list=ELNMuJvMLRRws
https://www.youtube.com/watch?v=1qNeGSJaQ9Q&t=4s
https://www.onceuponachef.com/recipes/best-ever-blueberry-muffins.html
https://www.nga.gov/collection/art-object-page.3276.html

https://nolanbyers.com/how-to-know-when-its-time-to-divorce-four-harbingers-of-bad-marriage/

https://www.justice.gov/opa/pr/opioid-manufacturer-purdue-pharma-pleads-guilty-fraud-and-kickback-conspiracies

https://culture.teldap.tw/culture/index.php?option=com_content&id=1155:meat-shaped-stone&Itemid=209

https://www.nsa.gov/Resources/Media-Destruction-Guidance/FAQs/

https://www.cureus.com/articles/37470-more-than-skin-deep-a-case-of-nevus-sebaceous-associated-with-basal-cell-carcinoma-transformation

https://nypost.com/2022/02/10/elon-musks-neuralink-allegedly-subjected-monkeys-to-extreme-suffering/

https://rarediseases.org/rare-diseases/schimmelpenning-syndrome/

https://www.medicinenet.com/involuntary_head_turning_or_twisting_muscle_twitching_painless_and_stiff_neck/multisymptoms.htm

https://whatis.techtarget.com/definition/daughterboard-or-daughter-board-daughter-card-or-daughtercard#:~:text=A%20daughterboard%20(or%20daughter%20board,circuitry%20of%20another%20circuit%20board.&text=A%20mezzanine%20card%20is%20a,second%20level%20above%20the%20motherboard.

https://medium.com/the-haven/top-ten-dead-presidents-ranked-by-penis-size-6fb1208184c3

http://www.earlychristianwritings.com/text/shepherd.html

https://medium.com/the-daily-ablutions/dime-novel-degenerate-1-kant-the-hard-boiled-detective-6bdfb89eeefa

https://www.loc.gov/item/99391599/

https://olemiss.edu/depts/general_library/archives/exhibits/past/ingrahamex/ingraham.html

http://www.nasonline.org/

https://www.biausa.org/brain-injury/about-brain-injury/basics/overview

https://users.clas.ufl.edu/burt/touchyfeelingsmaliciousobjects/Kristevapowersofhorrorabjection.pdf

https://www.health.harvard.edu/pain/7-faces-of-neck-pain

https://www.healthline.com/health/how-to-get-perky-boobs#:~:text=Exercises%20targeting%20your%20upper%20body,pound%20dumbbells%20with%20each%20exercise.

https://www.wikihow.com/Make-Your-Breasts-Perkier

https://www.quora.com/What-is-Omorashi

https://www.youtube.com/watch?v=rBp1Q_bHe0Y

https://www.nbcnews.com/news/world/dead-sea-scrolls-discoveries-are-first-ancient-bible-texts-be-n1261182

https://www.ranker.com/list/craziest-parts-of-the-gnostic-gospels/rachel-souerbry

https://www.indiatoday.in/magazine/offtrack/story/19980928-ancient-palm-leaf-manuscripts-are-in-danger-of-crumbling-away-827830-1998-09-28

https://www.skinnytaste.com/baked-chicken-parmesan/
https://skipmoen.com/2021/03/divine-pain/
https://newsroom.ucla.edu/releases/lost-memories-might-be-able-to-be-restored-new-ucla-study-indicates
https://time.com/3899789/lost-memories-retrieved/
https://en.wikipedia.org/wiki/Prometheus
https://www.siobeauty.com/blogs/news/marionette-lines
https://www.nbcnews.com/health/health-news/ugly-past-u-s-human-experiments-uncovered-flna1c9465329
http://news.bbc.co.uk/2/hi/programmes/file_on_4/4701196.stm
https://web.archive.org/web/20130425164618/http://www.hhs.gov/1946inoculationstudy/factsheet.html
https://www.pbs.org/kenburns/the-roosevelts/
https://www.cnn.com/interactive/2020/03/business/what-is-5g/index.html
https://www.pcmag.com/news/5g-conspiracy-theorists-are-embracing-new-wireless-technology-called-5g
https://www.biausa.org/brain-injury/about-brain-injury/nbiic/what-is-the-difference-between-an-acquired-brain-injury-and-a-traumatic-brain-injury
https://www.asha.org/students/speech-language-pathology/
https://en.wikipedia.org/wiki/Shoulder_angel#/media/File:Old_man_seated_and_writing_in_a_book,_an_angel_at_right_looking_over_his_shoulder,_after_Reni_(?)_MET_DP837921.jpg
https://www.mountsinai.org/locations/grabscheid-voice-swallowing-center/our-services/speech-language-pathology
https://www.boredpanda.com/hummingbird-wings-rainbow-christian-spencer/?page_numb=2&utm_source=google&utm_medium=organic&utm_campaign=organic
https://gurushots.com/article/15-beautiful-photos-of-birds-taking-flight
https://www.wherewomenwork.com/Career/1154/Inspiration-quotes-for-high-achieving-working-women
https://www.daveswordsofwisdom.com/2018/03/i-love-my-daughter.html
https://lassoa.com/collections/m35/products/to-my-daughter-be-brave-be-bold-be-beautiful-blanket
https://www.pinterest.com/pin/AWRTI4hV4HdGhRe0bszQaAe-Wzceycsr78H-E6IxLhEWY73VyVk6sic/
https://www.youtube.com/watch?v=T1g5tVGZhfk
https://lambdaliterary.org/2019/08/a-poem-by-stacy-skolnik/
https://thepinterestedparent.com/2018/03/mirror-mirror-on-the-wall-poem-printable/
https://www.youtube.com/watch?v=AN8-pNnvJ5s
https://en.wikipedia.org/wiki/His_Master%27s_Voice#/media/File:His_Master's_Voice.jpg
https://tenor.com/search/metamorphosis-gifs

https://www.scielo.br/j/anp/a/y65SG658xdTZWxtQmjmj9qd/?lang=en#:~:text=Psyche's%20mythological%20imagery%20in%20ancient,the%20shackles%20of%20the%20chrysalis.
https://www.inputmag.com/culture/let-sophia-the-robot-have-a-robot-baby
https://www.sleepfoundation.org/insomnia/what-causes-insomnia
https://www.ncbi.nlm.nih.gov/pmc/articles/PMC3402138/
https://www.nature.com/articles/d43747-020-00522-5
https://www.soulmachines.com/
https://www.ranker.com/list/rosemarys-baby-curse-facts/jacob-shelton
https://www.goodrx.com/well-being/healthy-aging/can-you-reverse-gray-hair
https://www.scientificamerican.com/article/mail-order-crispr-kits-allow-absolutely-anyone-to-hack-dna/
https://www.lifehack.org/804141/brain-exercises-for-memory
https://www.cognifit.com/?param1=adwords&param2=USA&gclid=Cj0KCQiAxoiQBhCRARIsAPsvo-w9rdImwjd-YKOiBqQUvjBx8ApJAB48-o3eJJNNKo7aCkDHOrv0oSsaAuCtEALw_wcB
https://www.youtube.com/watch?v=OkWVrLfiJKs
https://epicmychart.nychhc.org/MyChart/Authentication/Login?mode=stdfile&option=mchelp
https://www.npr.org/2021/09/01/1031053251/sackler-family-immunity-purdue-pharma-oxcyontin-opioid-epidemic
https://onlinelibrary.wiley.com/doi/full/10.1111/pops.12754
https://ilikemyteeth.org/fluoridation/fluoride-myths-facts/
https://goodmenproject.com/gender-sexuality/the-whole-man-balancing-logos-and-eros-dg/
https://www.rainn.org/articles/flashbacks
https://www.mayoclinic.org/diseases-conditions/post-traumatic-stress-disorder/symptoms-causes/syc-20355967
https://genius.com/Elvis-presley-shake-rattle-and-roll-lyrics
https://laboriacuboniks.net/manifesto/xenofeminism-a-politics-for-alienation/
https://en.wikipedia.org/wiki/Bunny_ears_(disambiguation)
https://supervert.com/elibrary/georges-bataille/story-of-the-eye
https://personaltao.com/taoism/what-is-yin-yang/
https://www.oculus.com/blog/exercise-by-accident-vr-games-to-help-you-work-out-at-home/
https://www.businessinsider.com/true-government-conspiracies-2013-12
https://en.wikipedia.org/wiki/Eurasian_skylark#In_culture
https://upload.wikimedia.org/wikipedia/en/e/e6/Toskylark.jpg
https://foreverbride.com/inspiration/health-and-beauty/personal-experience-getting-rid-forehead-lines/
https://www.esteelauder.com/product/689/77491/Product-Catalog/Skincare/Repair-Serum/Advanced-Night-Repair-Serum/Synchronized-Multi-Recovery-Complex?size=1.0_oz.&gclid=CjwKCAiA6Y2QBhAtEi

wAGHybPTetVl8wjqf7OatSNxw4gir9nhjzYVemiWPH0yf3ifT7Os4FX
wSRKxoCrIIQAvD_BwE&gclsrc=aw.ds
https://medcraveonline.com/JPCPY/the-psychopathology-of-fetishism-and-body-integrity-dysphoria-bid.html
https://www.newsnationnow.com/morninginamerica/tiktok-mental-disorder-trend/
https://medshadow.org/anesthesia-side-effects/
https://www.cjr.org/the_feature/the_fabulist_who_changed_journalism.php
http://www.todayifoundout.com/index.php/2013/09/one-shocking-cia-programs-time-project-mkultra/
https://web.archive.org/web/20160309202304/http://www.cs.berkeley.edu/~christos/classics/Deutsch_quantum_theory.pdf
https://www.sciencedaily.com/releases/2011/08/110803102844.htm
https://www.technologyreview.com/2010/12/13/198463/astronomers-find-first-evidence-of-other-universes/
https://dc.fandom.com/wiki/Metropolis
https://www.aaai.org/
https://www.cser.ac.uk/
https://www.theguardian.com/technology/2018/may/06/no-death-and-an-enhanced-life-is-the-future-transhuman
https://www.jstor.org/stable/283479
https://www.ricksnewyork.com/
https://www.lorealparisusa.com/beauty-magazine/skin-care/skin-care-concerns/how-to-get-rid-of-under-eye-bags
https://www.byrdie.com/microneedling-side-effects
https://www.elle.com/beauty/makeup-skin-care/a12773502/microneedling-faq-facts-cost/
http://classics.mit.edu/Plutarch/theseus.html
https://looserounds.com/2020/06/10/when-women-are-outlawed-only-fem-bots-will-work-in-vegas-brothels/
https://futurism.com/chatbot-abuse
https://www.youtube.com/playlist?app=desktop&list=PLAGggYDwCYhNUrPu-Pv7oBnNuCjDwH2WN
https://www.theguardian.com/technology/2020/jan/13/what-are-deepfakes-and-how-can-you-spot-them
https://www.youtube.com/watch?v=JoUWNBcBKkA
https://dc.fandom.com/wiki/Batman_Vol_1_8?file=Batman+8.jpg
https://en.wikipedia.org/wiki/Cartesian_theater#/media/File:Cartesian_Theater.svg
https://www.fragrantica.com/perfume/Revlon/Jean-Nate-9025.html
https://en.wikipedia.org/wiki/Self-similarity#/media/File:KochSnowGif16_800x500_2.gif
https://www.frontiersin.org/articles/10.3389/fnhum.2016.00105/full#:~:text=The%20alien%20hand%20syndrome%20(AHS,the%20intention%20of%20the%20patient.
https://www.youtube.com/watch?v=1qNeGSJaQ9Q

https://www.bbc.com/news/technology-30290540
https://us.norton.com/internetsecurity-how-to-how-can-i-access-the-deep-web.html
https://www.avast.com/c-dark-web#gref
https://en.wikipedia.org/wiki/Cynicism_(philosophy)
https://www.youtube.com/watch?v=ExGZtlzL1x4
https://www.youtube.com/watch?v=3lxp7WVXiXU
https://www.reddit.com/r/singularity/comments/pe5ilb/would_humans_even_have_a_purpose_in_an_ai/
https://waitbutwhy.com/2015/01/artificial-intelligence-revolution-1.html
https://www.smh.com.au/culture/books/dark-side-of-venus-goddess-represents-more-than-nudity-romance-and-sex-20191115-p53b0h.html
https://www.wikiart.org/en/toyen/a-girl-sleeping-under-the-stars-1944
https://mythologian.net/gaia-mother-earth-the-mother-of-all/
https://suplaney.files.wordpress.com/2010/09/foucault-the-history-of-sexuality-volume-1.pdf
https://www.youtube.com/watch?v=HaqjSCx_3uw
https://www.libraryofsocialscience.com/assets/pdf/freud_beyond_the_pleasure_principle.pdf
https://anythingthatmovestaxidermy.com/field-care.html
https://www.popsugar.com/celebrity/How-Did-Elvis-Priscilla-Presley-Meet-46501528
https://www.youtube.com/watch?v=JFXLNQleNrI
https://comicnewbies.com/2021/02/04/superman-fights-off-mind-control-injustice-gods-among-us/
https://www.phoenixhouse.org/
https://tvtropes.org/pmwiki/pmwiki.php/ComicBook/AMindSwitchInTime
https://www.youtube.com/watch?v=1Uw0xB_h3MY
https://blog.breathingcolor.com/photoshop-spot-healing-brush/
https://interestingliterature.com/2021/04/phoenix-symbolism-in-literature-and-myth/
https://www.discovermagazine.com/mind/the-man-who-tried-to-weigh-the-soul
https://screenrant.com/cyborg-superman-comic-origin-powers-explained/
https://www.leadinglady.com/blogs/archive/4-ways-to-naturally-lift-your-breasts
https://www.discovermagazine.com/mind/the-sense-of-smell-in-humans-is-more-powerful-than-we-think
https://www.scientificamerican.com/article/why-do-smells-trigger-memories1/
https://www.youtube.com/watch?v=_djxH-q0e48
https://www.amazon.com/Mars-Women-Venus-Communication-Relationships/dp/006016848
https://everything.explained.today/Hiereiai/

https://www.youtube.com/watch?v=gj0Rz-uP4Mk
https://clockwisestrippers.wordpress.com/2010/08/14/weird-things-strippers-do-clack-clack/
https://en.wikipedia.org/wiki/Oedipus_Rex#Fulfilling_prophecy
https://www.nytimes.com/1997/12/06/theater/how-oedipus-is-losing-his-complex.html
http://www.seasideaquarium.com/razorClams_page2.php
http://factmyth.com/factoids/a-soul-has-weight/
https://www.reuters.com/article/us-health-breathing-pen/forget-about-saving-a-life-by-plunging-a-pen-through-the-neck-idUSKCN0XP32Q
https://www.philosophy.com/hope-in-a-jar-smooth-glow-multi-tasking-moisturizer-2022.html?cgid=C112
https://www.sfu.ca/~andrewf/CONCEPT2.html
https://theculturetrip.com/north-america/mexico/articles/heres-why-the-aztec-death-whistle-is-mexicos-most-terrifying-musical-instrument/
https://www.rorschach.org/
https://psycho-tests.com/test/rorschach-inkblot
https://www.fda.gov/animal-veterinary/animal-health-literacy/all-about-bse-mad-cow-disease
https://www.youtube.com/watch?v=wTsp9A7OaBI
https://www.imdb.com/title/tt0383050/plotsummary?ref_=tt_ov_pl
https://www.youtube.com/watch?v=WyenVogM7-M
http://iama.stupid.cow.org/Audio/Halloween/Selections%20from%20The%20Haunted%20House%20and%20Other%20Spooky%20Poems%20and%20Tales%20(1970)/09%20The%20Velvet%20Ribbon.mp3
https://sites.pitt.edu/~dash/grimm012a.html
https://upload.wikimedia.org/wikipedia/commons/6/6d/The_Garden_of_Earthly_Delights_by_Bosch_High_Resolution.jpg
https://www.reddit.com/r/Buddhism/comments/liiv41/the_curious_case_of_the_conscious_corpse/
https://www.healthline.com/health/crackling-in-ear#:~:text=Eustachian%20tube%20dysfunction%20happens%20when,or%20congestion%20in%20your%20ear
https://www.hopkinsmedicine.org/health/conditions-and-diseases/aphasia
https://www.sciencedirect.com/topics/medicine-and-dentistry/waxy-flexibility
https://www.sleepfoundation.org/how-sleep-works/how-much-sleep-do-we-really-need
https://www.xnxx.com/search/daddy%20fetish%20daughter
https://www.crsd.org/cms/lib/PA01000188/Centricity/Domain/667/English/Fairy%20Tales/Fathers%20and%20Daughters.pdf
https://www.staples.com/uni-ball-Roller-Pen-Fine-Point-Black-12-pk-60101/product_132340?ci_sku=132340&KPID=132340&cid=PS:GS:SBD:PLA:OS&gclid=Cj0KCQiAxoiQBhCRARIsAPsvo-yNb4lLjoe1lFl7qjtzQIczpt0g3O81wEfGnNbJ2tVxyOW1R1XOmXEaAqtmEALw_wcB

https://archive.org/details/philosophicalbab00alis
https://cpb-us-e1.wpmucdn.com/blogs.uoregon.edu/dist/4/2521/files/2013/03/Taylor-Hodges-Kohanyi_2003-2b6wdel.pdf
https://www.genome.gov/genetics-glossary/Mutation
https://www.inverse.com/mind-body/how-to-reverse-false-memories-study
https://www.telegraph.co.uk/news/2016/09/20/are-you-living-in-an-alternate-reality-welcome-to-the-wacky-worl/
https://pubmed.ncbi.nlm.nih.gov/28613592/
https://www.vox.com/science-and-health/2018/4/20/17109764/deepfake-ai-false-memory-psychology-mandela-effect
https://www.manet.org/dead-christ-with-angels.jsp
https://www.alignmentforum.org/posts/qYzqDtoQaZ3eDDyxa/distinguishing-ai-takeover-scenarios
https://jetpress.org/volume1/moravec.htm
https://mychart.mountsinai.org/mychart/Authentication/Login?utm%5Fsource=mountsinaiorg&utm%5Fmedium=mychart&utm%5Fcampaign=msorghp&%5Fga=2%2E7170673%2E25645858%2E1644371743%2D1797971268%2E1643387551
https://pubmed.ncbi.nlm.nih.gov/28613592/
https://www.google.com/search?q=compound+pharmacy+near+me&oq=compound+pharmacy+near+me&aqs=chrome..69i57j0i40l2l2j0i512j0i22i30l6.7508j1j9&sourceid=chrome&ie=UTF-8
https://thevalemagazine.com/2019/11/06/agnes-richter-asylum-straitjacket/
https://www.collinsdictionary.com/us/dictionary/english/harbinger
https://www.metopera.org/season/tickets/
https://variety.com/2021/music/news/controlling-britney-spears-documentary-conservatorship-surveillance-phone-monitored-1235074025/
https://www.guggenheim.org/artwork/1311
https://www.state.gov/bureaus-offices/under-secretary-for-management/bureau-of-medical-services/
https://www.bbvaopenmind.com/en/science/leading-figures/what-remains-of-lamarck/
https://www.wanttoknow.info/mindcontrol?gclid=CjwKCAiA6Y2QBhAtEiwAGHybPahfJgycOKDK_ZLWY2vVRqwOQMR-n971QxqaGYIy0wZf_7bfD3QLahoCFAMQAvD_BwE
https://intelligence.org/about/
https://military-history.fandom.com/wiki/John_von_Neumann
https://www.nps.gov/sahi/index.htm
https://trulyexperiences.com/blog/fluorite-crystal/
http://mrsblueeyes123.com/
https://www.heretohelp.bc.ca/q-and-a/what-is-a-prodrome
https://www.youtube.com/watch?v=0Ld4INtDlN8
https://www.youtube.com/watch?v=VXIYGaqduyQ
https://www.informit.com/articles/article.aspx?p=170498

https://turbofuture.com/computers/the-motherboard-components
https://njmonline.nl/getpdf.php?id=1392
https://www.nationalgallery.org.uk/paintings/glossary/gabriel-archangel
https://en.wikipedia.org/wiki/Gabriel%27s_Horn
https://www.youtube.com/watch?v=SeMS8QEYIQU
https://en.wikipedia.org/wiki/Technological_singularity#/media/File:Major_Evolutionary_Transitions_digital.jpg
https://www.newyorker.com/tech/annals-of-technology/ada-lovelace-the-first-tech-visionary
https://www.outdoorlife.com/13-toxic-wild-plants-not-food/
https://www.youtube.com/watch?v=Q72KDDMnjp4
https://www.healthline.com/health/side-effects-of-general-anesthesia#longterm-side-effects
https://www.sun.org/encyclopedia/degeneracy
https://bigthink.com/health/psychology-of-foot-fetishes/
https://www.betterhelp.com/advice/general/understanding-imprinting-psychology/
https://www.goodmorningamerica.com/wellness/story/experts-troubled-tiktok-trend-teens-believing-mental-disorders-81964649
https://us.gamesplanet.com/game/super-seducer-3-uncensored-edition-download--4460-1
https://www.space.com/artemis-program.html
https://www.kennedyspacecenter.com/blog/what-is-the-artemis-program
https://www.samhsa.gov/find-help/national-helpline
https://www.express.co.uk/news/uk/1551868/Chimpanzee-attack-news-woman-face-ripped-off-Missouri-Chimpanzee-Sanctuary
https://ieeexplore.ieee.org/abstract/document/9144516
https://pubmed.ncbi.nlm.nih.gov/9814721/
https://books.google.com/books/about/Eros_in_Antiquity.html?id=McaZQgAACAAJ&source=kp_book_description
https://plato.stanford.edu/entries/pseudo-science/
https://quackwatch.org/related/PhonyAds/adindex/
https://www.vice.com/en/article/xgdq87/deepfakes-japan-arrest-japanese-porn
https://news.gallup.com/poll/16915/three-four-americans-believe-paranormal.aspx
https://matrixtherapypt.com/emotional-release/
https://somaticmovementcenter.com/muscle-memory-and-sensory-motor-amnesia/
https://psychosocialsomatic.com/trauma-and-the-psoas-muscle/
https://www.genome.gov/genetics-glossary/CRISPR#:~:text=CRISPR%20(short%20for%20"clustered%20regularly,editing%20systems%20found%20in%20bacteria.
https://www.britannica.com/event/Salem-witch-trials/The-trials

https://jacobinmag.com/2020/01/ronald-reagan-october-surprise-carter-iran-hostage-crisis-conspiracy
https://life-care-wellness.com/how-to-release-trauma-trapped-in-the-body/
https://quarterlife.org/blog/2016/11/11/20-tips-to-release-stress-and-heal-trauma-from-this-election
https://www.mayoclinichealthsystem.org/hometown-health/speaking-of-health/aphasia-putting-the-disorder-into-words
https://www.businessinsider.com/scientists-fake-news-and-disinformation-pseudoscience-2016-12
https://www.merriam-webster.com/dictionary/lachrymose
https://www.youtube.com/watch?v=6lnoM25D-js
https://www.google.com/search?q=peace+frog+lyrics&oq=Peace+frog+lyrics&aqs=chrome.0.0i512l2j0i22i30l7.192j0j7&sourceid=chrome&ie=UTF-8
https://www.telegraph.co.uk/technology/2016/06/02/elon-musk-become-cyborgs-or-risk-humans-being-turned-into-robots/
https://www.nbcnews.com/mach/science/tiny-tortoise-has-big-lesson-teach-kids-about-robots-ncna859571
http://www.f.waseda.jp/sidoli/Tiptree_Girl_Plugged_In.pdf
https://www.aivo.co/blog/are-robots-becoming-human-or-are-humans-becoming-robots
https://neuralink.com/blog/first-clinical-trial-open-for-recruitment/
https://www.youtube.com/watch?v=WnBjYpRYutE
https://www.youtube.com/watch?v=D3PtmUMqO58
https://wayback.archive-it.org/all/20081002044708/http://nat.org/sexbots.pdf
http://sorayama.jp/works/
http://www.p-synd.com/winterrose/technosexuality.html
https://my-name-is-apollo.tumblr.com/post/176988593369/a-g-a-l-m-a-t-o-p-h-i-l-i-a-phoebus-apollo
https://www.psychologytoday.com/us/blog/in-excess/201311/love-sculpture#:~:text=Agalmatophilia%20is%20a%20sexual%20paraphilia,other%20similar%20body%20shaped%20objects.&text=Agalmatophilia%20can%20also%20include%20'Pygmalionism,object%20of%20one's%20own%20creation.
https://www.esquire.com/lifestyle/a25018920/japan-married-hologram-gatebox/
https://campaignagainstsexrobots.org/
https://deepmind.com/
https://askanydifference.com/difference-between-fact-and-fiction/
https://www.buzzworthy.com/15-conspiracies-that-turned-out-to-be-true/
https://www.themuse.com/advice/5-different-types-of-imposter-syndrome-and-5-ways-to-battle-each-one
https://moviecultists.com/how-to-make-my-breast-perkier-naturally

https://www.edenbrothers.com/store/mix-celosia-seeds.html?gclid=Cj0KCQiAjJOQBhCkARIsAEKMtO0FgLfg9yM0P2oNXxGjw1OmIqcGCy6myQi9XzYLwUOZcQGtoVx5wJ0aAvfmEALw_wcB
https://www.science.org/content/article/black-hole
http://websites.umich.edu/~umfandsf/symbolismproject/symbolism.html/F/fire.html
https://www.britannica.com/topic/Sisyphus
https://www.theatlantic.com/national/archive/2013/10/how-spot-reptilians-runing-us-government/354496/
https://www.librarything.com/work/1670335
https://www.amazon.com/Access-Denied-Reasons-National-Security/dp/096601653X
https://www.youtube.com/watch?v=DMH5WgGFxlc
https://www.nytimes.com/packages/pdf/national/13inmate_ProjectMKULTRA.pdf
https://www.smithsonianmag.com/science-nature/mathematical-madness-mobius-strips-and-other-one-sided-objects-180970394/
https://kashgar.com.au/blogs/gods-goddesses/the-hindu-god-ganesh-who-is-this-elephant-headed-deity-anyway
https://www.artofliving.org/wisdom/knowledge-sheets/symbolism-ganesha
http://www.pure-spirit.com/more-animal-symbolism/400-owl#:~:text=Rather%20than%20intellectual%20wisdom%2C%20though,the%20wisdom%20of%20the%20soul.&text=Even%20the%20mythology%20relates%20owl,gave%20their%20pantheon%20human%20forms.
https://www.spiritanimal.info/wolf-spirit-animal/
https://crystalclearintuition.com/owl-meaning/
https://www.bbc.co.uk/teach/alan-turing-creator-of-modern-computing/zhwp7nb
https://web.archive.org/web/20140714220221/http://cosmosmagazine.com/news/something-big-found-beyond-edge-universe/
https://phys.org/news/2014-12-universe-dimensions.html
https://aeon.co/essays/how-many-dimensions-are-there-and-what-do-they-do-to-reality
https://cendrines.com/what-does-it-mean-to-be-a-multi-dimensional-being/
https://www.sciencefocus.com/science/do-two-mirrors-facing-each-other-produce-infinite-reflections/
https://slate.com/technology/2015/04/elephants-have-great-memory-and-learning-skills-but-are-they-self-aware.html
https://whatistranshumanism.org/
https://www.writerswrite.co.za/10-ways-to-kick-start-your-writing-at-halloween/
https://www.stopkillerrobots.org/stop-killer-robots/emerging-tech-and-artificial-intelligence/

https://www.pewresearch.org/fact-tank/2017/10/04/6-key-findings-on-how-americans-see-the-rise-of-automation/
https://builtin.com/robotics
https://stanfordhealthcare.org/medical-conditions/skin-hair-and-nails/burns/stages.html
https://www.livescience.com/63645-optical-illusion-young-old-woman.html
https://en.wikipedia.org/wiki/Catharsis
https://www.intechopen.com/chapters/53880
https://answersingenesis.org/bible-questions/tree-knowledge-good-and-evil/
https://ideologicorgan.bandcamp.com/album/images-of-the-dream-and-death\
http://mindjustice.org/2003_survey.htm
https://www.hanacure.com/?gclid=Cj0KCQiAgP6PBhDmARIsAPWMq6mZI2odk6yeb8evE9Em0jf9pBq0Gvp3Byo9yvThelsusy26eR5q4hQaArWREALw_wcB
https://www.npr.org/templates/story/story.php?storyId=5168026
https://web.archive.org/web/20071013040110/http://www.royalsoc.ac.uk/news.asp?year=&id=4298
https://www.ncbi.nlm.nih.gov/pmc/articles/PMC4488611/
https://www.simplyrecipes.com/recipes/banana_bread/
https://www.fbi.gov/history/famous-cases/velvalee-dickinson-the-doll-woman
https://www.cosmopolitan.com/style-beauty/news/a30238/teen-human-barbie-claims-she-is-the-best-one-yet/
http://www.dreambible.com/search.php?q=Murder
https://www.learning-mind.com/dreams-about-murder/
https://www.nytimes.com/2017/12/16/us/politics/pentagon-program-ufo-harry-reid.html
https://www.iherb.com/pr/tiger-balm-pain-relieving-ointment-extra-strength-63-oz-18-g/6787?gclid=Cj0KCQiAxoiQBhCRARIsAPsvoykLL44OAO_EgsZsWbCEokKOTvX0d0WN4TfR19iJUndKfnWaLJJOQgaAkRqEALw_wcB
https://www.bladderandbowel.org/bowel/bowel-treatments/8-methods-encourage-bowel-movement/
https://www.yourgenome.org/facts/what-is-a-mutation
https://www.ncbi.nlm.nih.gov/pmc/articles/PMC2292429/
https://www.forensicscolleges.com/blog/resources/10-signs-someone-is-lying
https://www.forbes.com/sites/alisonescalante/2021/02/10/research-finds-a-new-trick-to-telling-if-someone-is-lying-their-voice/?sh=779dc21d42ad
https://forums.somethingawful.com/showthread.php?threadid=3969431&userid=0&perpage=40&pagenumber=4
https://www.reddit.com/r/MandelaEffect/comments/64d67b/can_anybody_find_a_vehicle_with_a_mirror_saying/

https://www.gutenberg.org/files/159/159-h/159-h.htm
https://i.kym-cdn.com/photos/images/original/001/202/629/57c.png
https://www.livescience.com/62234-prosthetic-memory-neural-implant.html
https://en.wikipedia.org/wiki/Uplift_(science_fiction)
https://web.archive.org/web/20200227040232/https://pdfs.semanticscholar.org/d526/2b894abffcb2bd5389c06af018799b82a118.pdf
https://www.youtube.com/watch?v=wbwuxoYBR4o
https://link.springer.com/article/10.3758/BF03196385
https://www.smithsonianmag.com/science-nature/how-tuberculosis-shaped-victorian-fashion-180959029/
https://futurism.com/a-new-device-could-make-memory-implants-a-reality
https://www.frontiersin.org/articles/10.3389/fnins.2017.00584/full
https://www.gulfcoasthairrestoration.com/shock-hair-loss-why-does-it-occur-is-it-permanent/
https://www.yetkinbayer.com/en/what-is-shock-loss.html
https://www.housedigest.com/644515/the-tiktok-grout-cleaning-hack-the-internet-is-obsessed-with/
https://www.pewresearch.org/internet/2018/12/10/artificial-intelligence-and-the-future-of-humans/
https://www.crssny.com/
https://www.ncbi.nlm.nih.gov/pmc/articles/PMC6443620/
https://web.archive.org/web/20130713145805/http://www.gwu.edu/~nsarchiv/radiation/dir/mstreet/commeet/meet4/trnsct04.txt
http://content.time.com/time/specials/packages/article/0,28804,1860871_1860876_1861029,00.html
https://www.liquor.com/recipes/mind-eraser/
https://www.nei.nih.gov/learn-about-eye-health/eye-conditions-and-diseases/floaters
https://www.learnreligions.com/ouroboros-4123019
https://mindmatters.ai/2019/10/anti-technology-backlash-whats-real-whats-myth/
https://theconversation.com/super-intelligence-and-eternal-life-transhumanisms-faithful-follow-it-blindly-into-a-future-for-the-elite-78538
https://www.computerworld.com/article/3005204/ban-the-killer-robots-movement-could-backfire.html
https://www.nigms.nih.gov/education/fact-sheets/Pages/burns.aspx
https://www.discovermagazine.com/the-sciences/earth-has-been-hiding-a-fifth-layer-in-its-inner-core
https://www.forbes.com/sites/trevornace/2016/01/16/layers-of-the-earth-lies-beneath-earths-crust/?sh=54e4b3f5441d
https://sites.pitt.edu/~dash/type0510b.html
https://en.wikipedia.org/wiki/Montreal_experiments
https://www.wikihow.com/Activate-Dried-Yeast

https://www.thenewatlantis.com/publications/understanding-heidegger-on-technology

https://www.pregnancybirthbaby.org.au/umbilical-care#:~:text=In%20the%20womb%2C%20the%20umbilical,to%20prevent%20problems%20during%20healing.

https://news.berkeley.edu/2011/09/22/brain-movies/

https://www.youtube.com/watch?v=u_sY-nJ179U

https://www.britannica.com/topic/Cartesianism

https://www.mindbodygreen.com/articles/best-shower-cleaners

https://www.urbandictionary.com/define.php?term=there%27s%20no%20there%20there

https://www.vox.com/science-and-health/20978285/optical-illusion-science-humility-reality-polarization

https://www.ncbi.nlm.nih.gov/pmc/articles/PMC4297672/

http://home.uchicago.edu/~jlear/docs/katharsis.pdf

https://repository.up.ac.za/bitstream/handle/2263/11494/VanTongeren_Nietzsche%282001%29.pdf?sequence=1

https://www.worldwidewords.org/weirdwords/ww-sop1.htm

https://www.aamc.org/news-insights/what-informed-consent-really-means